CONOR McPHERSO.

Conor McPherson was b   ... Plays include
Rum and Vodka (Fly by N   ~ Co., Dublin); *The Good
Thief* (Dublin Theatre Festival; Stewart Parker Award); *This Lime
Tree Bower* (Fly by Night Theatre Co. and Bush Theatre,
London; Meyer-Whitworth Award); *St Nicholas* (Bush Theatre
and Primary Stages, New York); *The Weir* (Royal Court, London,
Duke of York's, West End and Walter Kerr Theatre, New York;
Laurence Olivier, Evening Standard, Critics' Circle, George
Devine Awards); *Dublin Carol* (Royal Court and Atlantic
Theater, New York); *Port Authority* (Ambassadors Theatre, West
End, Gate Theatre, Dublin and Atlantic Theater, New York);
Shining City (Royal Court, Gate Theatre, Dublin and Manhattan
Theatre Club, New York; Tony Award nomination for Best Play);
The Seafarer (National Theatre, London, Abbey Theatre, Dublin
and Booth Theater, New York; Laurence Olivier, Evening
Standard, Tony Award nominations for Best Play); *The Veil*
(National Theatre) and *The Night Alive* (Donmar Warehouse and
Atlantic Theater, New York; New York Drama Critics' Circle
Award for Best New Play). Theatre adaptations include Daphne
du Maurier's *The Birds* (Gate Theatre, Dublin and Guthrie
Theater, Minneapolis) and August Strindberg's *The Dance of
Death* (Donmar at Trafalgar Studios).

Work for the cinema includes *I Went Down*, *Saltwater*, Samuel
Beckett's *Endgame*, *The Actors*, and *The Eclipse*. He also
adapted John Banville's *Elegy for April* for the BBC.

Awards for his screenwriting include three Best Screenplay
Awards from the Irish Film and Television Academy; Spanish
Cinema Writers Circle Best Screenplay Award; the CICAE
Award for Best Film Berlin Film festival; Jury Prize San
Sebastian Film Festival; and the Méliès d'Argent Award for
Best European Film.

Other Titles in this Series

Conor McPherson

PLAYS: TWO

The Weir
Dublin Carol
Port Authority
Come On Over

with an Afterword by the Author

NICK HERN BOOKS
London
www.nickhernbooks.co.uk

A Nick Hern Book

McPherson Plays: Two first published in Great Britain as a paperback original in 2004 by Nick Hern Books Limited, The Glasshouse, 49a Goldhawk Road London W12 8QP

Reprinted 2010, 2012, 2014

Cover image: Conor McPherson

Typeset by Country Setting, Kingsdown, Kent
Printed in Great Britain by CPI Group (UK) Ltd

A CIP catalogue record for this book is available from the British Library

ISBN 978 1 85459 777 9

For the actors

Contents

THE WEIR

The Weir was first performed at the Royal Court Theatre Upstairs, West Street, London, on 4 July 1997. The cast was as follows:

JIM	Kieran Ahern
BRENDAN	Brendan Coyle
VALERIE	Julia Ford
FINBAR	Gerard Horan
JACK	Jim Norton

Director   Ian Rickson
Designer   Rae Smith
Lighting Designer   Paule Constable
Music   Stephen Warbeck

The production transferred to the Royal Court Theatre Downstairs, St Martin's Lane, London, on 18 February 1998 where it played for two years with successive cast changes.

Characters

JACK, *fifties*

BRENDAN, *thirties*

JIM, *forties*

FINBAR, *late forties*

VALERIE, *thirties*

The play is set in a rural part of Ireland, Northwest Leitrim or Sligo. Present day. Stage setting: a small rural bar.

A counter, left, with three bar taps. The spirits are not mounted, simply left on the shelf. There are three stools at the counter.

There is a fireplace, right. There is a stove built into it. Near this is a low table with some small stools and a bigger, more comfortable chair, nearest the fire. There is another small table, front, with a stool or two.

On the wall, back, are some old black and white photographs: a ruined abbey; people posing near a newly erected ESB weir; a town in a cove with mountains around it.

An old television is mounted up in a corner. There is a small radio on a shelf behind the bar.

A door, right, is the main entrance to the bar. A door, back, leads to the toilets and a yard.

This bar is part of a house and the house is part of a farm.

The door, right, opens. JACK comes in. He wears a suit which looks a bit big for him, and a white shirt open at the collar. Over this is a dirty anorak. He takes the anorak off and hangs it up. He wipes his boots aggressively on a mat.

He goes behind the counter. He selects a glass and goes to pour himself a pint of stout. Nothing comes out of the tap. He vainly tries it again and looks underneath the counter. He turns and takes a bottle from the shelf, awkwardly prising off the top. He pours it and leaves it on the bar to settle. He turns to the till which he opens with practised, if uncertain, ease. He takes a list of prices from beside the till and holds a pair of spectacles up to his face while he examines it. He puts money in the till and takes his change.

As he finishes this, the door at back opens. BRENDAN comes in. He wears a sweater, heavy cord pants and a pair of slip-on shoes. He carries a bucket with peat briquettes. He goes to the fireplace, barely acknowledging JACK, just his voice.

BRENDAN. Jack.

JACK. Brendan. (*Lifting glass.*) What's with the Guinness?

BRENDAN (*putting peat in the stove*). I don't know. It's the power in the tap. It's a new barrel and everything.

JACK. Is the Harp one okay?

BRENDAN. Yeah.

JACK. Well, would you not switch them around and let a man have a pint of stout, no?

BRENDAN. What about the Harp drinkers?

JACK (*derision*). 'The Harp drinkers.'

BRENDAN. Your man's coming in to do it in the morning. Have a bottle.

JACK. I'm having a bottle. (*Pause.*) I'm not happy about it, now mind, right? But, like.

They laugh.

BRENDAN. Go on out of that.

JACK (*drinks*). What the hell. Good for the worms.

BRENDAN. I'd say you have a right couple of worms, alright.

They laugh. Pause. BRENDAN *stands wiping his hands.*

That's some wind, isn't it?

JACK. It is.

BRENDAN. Must have been against you, was it?

JACK *comes out from behind the counter.*

JACK. It was. It was against me 'til I came around the Knock. It was a bit of shelter then.

BRENDAN *goes in behind the counter. He tidies up, dries glasses.*

BRENDAN. Yeah it's a funny one. It's coming from the North.

JACK. Mm. Ah, it's mild enough though.

BRENDAN. Ah yeah. It's balmy enough. (*Pause.*) It's balmy enough.

JACK. Were you in Carrick today?

BRENDAN. I wasn't, no. I had the sisters over doing their rounds. Checking up on me.

JACK. Checking their investments.

BRENDAN. Oh yeah. 'Course, they don't have a fucking clue what they're looking for, d'you know? They're just vaguely . . . you know.

JACK. Keeping the pressure on you.

BRENDAN. This is it. (*Pause.*) At me to sell the top field.

JACK. You don't use it much.

BRENDAN. No. No I don't. Too much trouble driving a herd up. But I know they're looking at it, all they see is new cars for the hubbies, you know?

JACK. Mm. You're not just trying to spite them? Get them vexed, ha?

BRENDAN. Not at all. I'm, just. It's a grand spot up there. Ah, I don't know. Just . . .

Short pause.

JACK. They over the whole day?

BRENDAN. They got here about two. They'd gone for lunch in the Arms. Got their story straight. Ah they were gone and all about half four.

JACK. They've no attachment to the place, no?

BRENDAN. No they don't. They look around, and it's . . . 'Ah yeah . . . ' you know?

They laugh a little.

It's gas.

JACK. Mm.

BRENDAN. Were you in Carrick yourself?

JACK. I was. Flew in about eleven, threw on a fast bet. Jimmy was there, we went for a quick one in the Pot.

BRENDAN. How is he? And the ma?

JACK. Ah. Jimmy. Be in tonight. He put me on to a nice one. We got her at eleven to four.

BRENDAN. You're learning to listen, ha?

JACK. Ah. Fuck that sure. I know, but I've been having the worst run of shit you wouldn't believe. I was that desperate, I'd listen to anybody.

BRENDAN. Go on out of that.

JACK. Ah no. No no. Fair dues. I'll say it. He got us a right one. And it's good, you know. Break a streak like that.

BRENDAN. You're a user.

JACK (laughs). There's worse.

BRENDAN. Yeah. There might be.

JACK. But, ah, he was telling me. Did you know about Maura Nealon's house?

BRENDAN. No.

JACK. Well. Jim says he met Finbar Mack down in the Spar. Finally, either sold or's renting the, the thing, after how many years it's sat there?

BRENDAN. Jays, four or five in anyway.

JACK. Jim says five this month. And Finbar's going bananas with the great fella that he is. Patting himself on the back, goodo, and talking about the new resident. Who, he says, is a fine girl. Single. Down from Dublin and all this. And Finbar's nearly leaving the wife just to have a chance with this one. Only messing, like. But he's bringing her in here tonight, the nearest place. To old . . . Maura's. Bringing her in for a drink. Introduce her to the natives.

BRENDAN. The dirty bastard. I don't want him using in here for that sort of carry on. A married man like him.

JACK. Ah he's only old shit. He wouldn't have the nerve. Sure, how far'd he get anyway? The fucking head on him. He's only having a little thrill. Bringing her around. And I'll tell you what it is as well. He's coming in here with her. And he's the one. He's the one that's 'with' her, in whatever fucking . . . sense we're talking about. He's bringing her in. And there's you and me, and the Jimmy fella, the muggins's, the single fellas. And he's the married fella. And he's going 'Look at this! There's obviously something the fuck wrong with yous. Yous are single and you couldn't get a woman near this place. And look at me. I'm hitched. I'm over and done with, and I'm having to beat them off.'

BRENDAN. Yeah. That's the way cunts always go about their business. It's intrusive, it's bad manners, it's . . .

JACK. Ah, it's a juvenile carry on. You know?

BRENDAN. Mm.

JACK. Let her come in herself.

BRENDAN. Yeah. That'd be better. That'd make more sense, for fuck's sake.

JACK. Leave her be. Don't know if I'll stay actually.

BRENDAN. Mm.

Pause. JACK *drains his glass and puts it on the bar.*

JACK. Go on.

BRENDAN *takes the glass and pours a fresh bottle.*

Don't want to leave Jimmy in the lurch. You know? Trying to hold his own in the Finbar Mack world of big business.

They laugh a little.

BRENDAN. Fucking . . . Jimmy talking all that crack with Finbar.

JACK. That's the thing though. The Jimmy fella's got more going on up here (*Head.*) than popular opinion would give him credit for.

BRENDAN. Sure, don't we know too well for God's sake?

JACK. I know.

BRENDAN. We know only too well.

JACK *counts change out on the bar.*

JACK. Would you give us ten Silk Cut please, Brendan?

BRENDAN. Red?

JACK. Please.

BRENDAN *puts the cigarettes on the bar.*

Good man.

Pause. JACK *doesn't touch them yet.* BRENDAN *counts the money off the bar.* JACK *pauses before drinking.*

Are we right?

BRENDAN. Close enough. Cheers.

JACK. Good luck.

JACK *takes a long drink. Pause.*

I know I do be at you. I'll keep at you though.

BRENDAN. About what?

JACK. Don't be messing. Come on.

BRENDAN. Ah.

JACK. A youngfella like you. And this place a right going concern.

BRENDAN. Ah. The odd time. You know, the odd time I'd think about it.

JACK. You should though.

BRENDAN. Well then, so should you.

JACK. Would you go on? An auldfella like me!

BRENDAN. Would you listen to him?

JACK. Sure what would I want giving up my freedom?

BRENDAN. Well then me as well!

Pause.

JACK. Tch. Maybe. Maybe there's something to be said for the old independence.

BRENDAN. Ah there is.

Pause.

JACK. A lot to be said for it.

BRENDAN. Mm. (*Pause.*) Mm.

JACK. Cheers.

BRENDAN. Good luck.

JACK *takes a long drink. The main door opens and* JIM *enters. He takes off an anorak to reveal a festive-looking cardigan.* JACK *pretends not to notice him.*

JACK (*winks*). Oh yes, Brendan, the luck is changing. I got me and the Jimmy fella on to a nice one today. That fella'd want to listen to me a bit more often, I tell you.

JIM. I'm going to have to start charging you for tips, am I?

JACK. Ah James! What'll you have?

JIM. Teach you some manners. Teach him some manners, Brendan, ha? Small one please, Jack.

BRENDAN. Small one.

JACK. Sure it'd take more than money to put manners on me, ha Brendan?

BRENDAN. It'd take a bomb under you.

JACK. Now you said it. Bomb is right. That wind still up, Jim?

JIM. Oh it is, yeah. Warm enough though.

JACK. We were just saying.

BRENDAN. For a Northerly.

JIM. Oh that's from the West now.

BRENDAN. Is it?

JIM. Oh yeah that's a Westerly.

JACK. Must've shifted.

JIM. Mm.

Pause. JIM *comes to the bar.*

Thanking you.

JACK. Good luck.

JIM. Good luck.

BRENDAN. Good luck.

JACK *counts change out on the bar.*

JACK. Are we right?

BRENDAN *counts and pushes a coin back towards* JACK.

BRENDAN (*gathering coins*). Now we are. Sure it's hard enough to come by without giving it away.

JACK. This is it. Oh. (*To* JIM.) Are you doing anything tomorrow?

JIM. What time?

JACK. I have to get out to Conor Boland. His tractor's packed up. And I have Father Donal's jalopy in since Tuesday. Said I'd change the oil. Haven't done it yet. Would you ever come in and do it so I can get over to Boland's?

JIM. It'd have to be early. I'm dropping the mother out to Sligo.

JACK. Well, whatever. Is that alright?

JIM. Ah, it should be, yeah. Pint?

JACK. Not for the moment. You go on.

JIM. Pint please, Brendan. You on the bottles?

BRENDAN *takes a glass and pours* JIM *a pint of lager from the good tap.*

JACK. Ah. Medicinal.

JIM. Ha?

BRENDAN. Ah the tap's fucked.

JIM. I was wondering, 'Jaysus what's your man fucking doing now', you know?

BRENDAN. Yeah. He'd be the fella'd have a figary and be only drinking bottles from now on. He would. (*To* JACK.) You would. Be you to a fucking tee.

JACK *sits as though he has to bear the world with great patience. They laugh. Pause.* JACK *shakes his head.*

JACK. How's the mammy today?

JIM. Ah, you know?

JACK. Tch. I have to get down and see her. I keep saying it.

JIM (*tone of 'No rush. No pressure'*). Well whenever, whenever you want.

BRENDAN. Do you think you'll do anything?

JIM. About?

BRENDAN. About up there on your own and all that?

JIM. Ah. Sure where would I go? And I was talking to Finbar Mack. Be lucky to get twenty thousand for the place. Sure where would you be going with that? (*Short pause.*) You know?

JACK. With the acre?

JIM. Ah yeah, the whole . . . the whole thing.

JACK. Ah you're grand with the few little jobs around here.

JIM. Ah.

JACK. You'll be cosy enough.

Pause.

BRENDAN. Jack was telling me about Finbar. And the new eh . . .

JIM. Mmm, yeah. I was telling him earlier.

JACK. I was telling him.

JIM. I've seen her since.

BRENDAN. Oh yeah?

JIM. Yeah, they were in Finbar's car going up the Head.

JACK *and* BRENDAN *exchange a look.*

BRENDAN. Fucking hell.

JACK. Like a courting couple or something.

JIM. He's showing her the area.

JACK. Jesus. 'The area.' He's a terrible fucking thick. What the fuck, is he, doing? You know?

JIM. Ah. She's . . . This is the only place near to her.

JACK. She can . . . (*Nodding.*) find her own way surely, Jim, come on.

BRENDAN. Well it's, you know. If it's courtesy, which is one thing, and a business . . . act or whatever, you know, you have to say, well okay and . . . But if it's all messy, I'm trapped in here behind this fucking thing. And you wish he'd stop acting the mess. I have to respect whatever, they're . . .

JACK. Well this is it, we're here.

JIM. It's probably not really anything.

Short pause.

JACK. What age would she be, about, Jim?

JIM. Em. I only saw her for a sec. I'd say, (*Beat.*) like they were in the car and all. I'd say about thirties. Very nice looking.

Pause.

JACK. Dublin woman.

JIM. Dublin.

Short pause.

BRENDAN. She's no one in the area, no?

JIM. No she's . . . coming down, you know?

JACK. Mm. (*Pause.*) Yeah.

JIM. Good luck. (*Drinks.*)

JACK. Cheers. (*Drinks.*)

BRENDAN. Good luck, boys.

JACK. Another week or two now, you'll be seeing the first of the Germans.

BRENDAN. Mm. Stretch in the evening, yeah.

JACK. You still wouldn't think about clearing one of the fields for a few caravans.

BRENDAN. Ah.

JACK. The top field.

BRENDAN. Ah there wouldn't be a lot of shelter up there, Jack. There'd be a wind up there that'd cut you.

JIM. D'you know what you could do? The herd'd be grand up there, and you could, you know, down here.

BRENDAN. Ah. (*Short pause.*) They do be around anyway. You know yourself.

JIM. Ah, they do.

JACK. You're not chasing the extra revenue.

BRENDAN. Or the work!

JIM. They do be around right enough.

BRENDAN. I'll leave the campsites to Finbar, ha? He'll sort them out.

JACK. Ah, Finbar's in real need of a few shekels.

They laugh.

BRENDAN. Ah he's in dire need of a few bob, the poor fella, that's right, that's right.

JACK. Mm.

Pause.

BRENDAN. Yeah. If you had all . . . the families out there. On their holliers. And all the kids and all. You'd feel the evenings turning. When they'd be leaving. And whatever about how quiet it is now. It'd be fucking shocking quiet then. (*Short pause.*) You know?

Pause.

JACK. Mm.

JIM. D'you want a small one, Jack?

JACK. Go on.

JIM. Two small ones please, Brendan.

BRENDAN. The small fellas.

BRENDAN *works.* JIM *counts some change on to the bar.*

JACK. Are you having one yourself?

BRENDAN. I'm debating whether to have one.

JACK. Ah have one and don't be acting the mess.

BRENDAN. Go on then.

BRENDAN *pours himself a glass of whiskey.*

JACK. Good man. (*Counts change on to the bar.*) A few shekels, ha? (*They smile.*) Mm.

JACK *takes out his cigarettes.*

Jim?

JIM. Oh cheers Jack.

JIM *takes one.*

JACK. Brendan?

BRENDAN. Fags and all, ha?

JACK. Go on. They're good for you.

BRENDAN (*taking one*). Go on.

They light up from a match which JACK *strikes. They puff contentedly for a moment.*

JIM (*lifting glass*). Keep the chill out.

JACK. This is it. Cheers.

BRENDAN. Cheers men.

JIM. Good luck.

They drink.

JACK. Now.

JIM. D'yous hear a car?

Pause.

BRENDAN. No.

JIM. That's Finbar's car.

Pause.

He's parked.

JACK. I didn't see the lights.

JIM. He came around the Knock.

From off they hear FINBAR*'s voice.*

FINBAR (*off*). Ah yeah, sure half the townland used to nearly live in here.

JACK. There we are now.

The door opens and FINBAR *brings* VALERIE *in.*

FINBAR. That's it now.

FINBAR *wears a light cream coloured suit and an open collar.* VALERIE *wears jeans and a sweater. She carries a jacket.*

Men. This is Valerie. She's just moved into Maura Nealon's old house.

JACK. Hello, how are you?

JACK *shakes her hand.*

VALERIE. Hello.

FINBAR. This is Jack Mullen. He has a little garage up around the Knock.

JACK *nods politely.*

JACK. Now.

FINBAR. This is Jim Curran. Does a bit of work with Jack.

VALERIE *shakes hands with* JIM.

VALERIE. Pleased to meet you.

JIM. Pleased to meet you.

FINBAR. And this Brendan. Brendan Byrne.

VALERIE. Hello.

They shake hands.

BRENDAN. How are you?

FINBAR. This is his bar. And all the land I showed you. All back down the hill. That's all his farm.

VALERIE. Oh right. It's all lovely here.

BRENDAN. Oh yeah. It's a grand spot all along . . . for going for a walk or that, all down the cliffs.

FINBAR. Oh it's lovely all around here. What'll you have?

BRENDAN. Oh, I'll get this, Finbar. No. What, what do you want?

FINBAR. Oh now, ha ha. Eh, I'll have a pint then, what?, says you, if it's going, ha? Eh Harp please Brendan.

JACK *looks at* FINBAR. FINBAR *nods at him.*

Jack.

JACK. Finbar.

BRENDAN. What would you like, Valerie?

VALERIE. Em. Could I have . . . Do you have . . . em, a glass of white wine?

Pause.

BRENDAN (*going*). Yeah. I'm just going to run in the house.

VALERIE. Oh no. Don't. Don't put yourself to any trouble.

BRENDAN. No. No it's no trouble. I have a bottle.

BRENDAN *goes*.

FINBAR. He probably has a bottle of the old vino, from feckin . . . Christmas, ha?

JACK. It's not too often the . . . the . . . wine does be flowing in here.

VALERIE. I'm all embarrassed now.

FINBAR. Don't be silly. Sit up there now, and don't mind us. Don't mind these country fellas.

JACK. Jays. You're not long out of it yourself, says the man, ha?

FINBAR (*winks*). They're only jealous Valerie because I went the town to seek my fortune. And they all stayed out here on the bog picking their holes.

JACK. Janey, now, ha? You didn't have very far to seek. Just a quick look in Big Finbar's will, I think is more like it.

FINBAR. Big Finbar's will! That's shrewd investment, boy. That's an eye for the gap.

JACK. Yeah, he probably fleeced you on Maura Nealon's house, did he?

VALERIE. I have to say I don't think so.

FINBAR. Good girl.

VALERIE. But it's very reasonable all around here, isn't it?

FINBAR. Oh it is, yeah. You know . . .

Short pause.

JACK. Is there much doing up on it?

FINBAR. Ah, hardly any.

VALERIE (*checking with* FINBAR). There's one or two floor-boards. Bit of paint.

JACK (*indicating* JIM). Well, there's your man. If you're looking for a good pair of hands.

VALERIE. Is that right?

JIM. I'll have a look for you, if you like. I know that house.

FINBAR. Don't be charging her through the nose now.

JIM. Ah ha, now.

BRENDAN *returns with a bottle of wine.*

FINBAR. You'd want to be giving her a neighbourly . . . rate, now, is the thing, ha?

JIM. Oh yeah.

JACK. Would you listen to him? 'Neighbourly rates . . . ' Wasn't by giving neighbourly rates you bought half the fucking town.

FINBAR. Half the town! (*To* VALERIE, *winking.*) I bought the whole town. Eye for the gap, you see.

JACK. Eye for your gap is right.

FINBAR (*to* BRENDAN). How long has that been in there? Lying in some drawer . . .

BRENDAN (*corkscrewing the bottle*). Ah, it was a . . . present or some . . . (*Looks at label.*) 1990. Now. Vintage, ha?

They laugh.

I hope it's alright now.

VALERIE. It's grand. I won't know the difference.

They watch BRENDAN *open the bottle. He pours a tumbler-full, then holds it up to the light, then sniffs it.*

BRENDAN. I think it's alright.

FINBAR. Ah would you give the woman the feckin' thing. The tongue's hanging out of her.

Again they watch as VALERIE *takes the glass.*

VALERIE. Thanks Brendan.

They watch her drink.

That's gorgeous. I'm not joking now. That's lovely.

FINBAR. Good.

BRENDAN. I'm putting it in the fridge for you, Valerie. (*He does.*)

Pause. FINBAR *nods at* VALERIE, *a reassuring 'Hello'.*

FINBAR (*to* JACK *and* JIM). How d'yous do today, boys?

JACK. Are you codding me? With this fella? Eleven to four we got her at. Came down to six to four.

FINBAR. Sheer Delight, was it?

JACK. Yeah. Kenny down in the shop, the knacker. Adjusting everything how this fella's betting.

BRENDAN. Look who's talking.

JACK. Yeah right.

JIM. He hardly ever listens to me.

JACK. Well. Now . . .

FINBAR. He's too proud, Jimmy. Too proud to admit when he needs a tip off you.

JACK (*emphatically*). I . . . have . . . my policy on this. And I have my principle. I am the first one to say it about this fella. See, usually, Valerie, usually, not all the time, Jim's not too far off the mark.

FINBAR. 'Too far off the mark!' (*To* VALERIE.) He's bang on the nail.

BRENDAN *places a pint on the bar.*

Thanks Brendan. (*He puts his hand in his pocket.*)

JACK. Not every time. Jim.

BRENDAN *waves* FINBAR *away.*

FINBAR. Thanks, thanks a million. (*To* VALERIE.) He is.

JACK. Bang on the nail is one thing, from judgement . . . and . . . But, and Jimmy knows I don't mean anything by this, and I know because we've spoken about this before. He has a scientific approach. He studies the form. And, no offence, he has a bit of time to be doing that. He studies it Valerie, and fair play to him, right? Do you bet on horses?

VALERIE. No.

FINBAR. Good girl.

JACK. Well he, how much, Jim, would you make in a month? On the horses.

JIM. Ah it evens out Jack. Like I'm not eh . . . I don't . . .

JACK. How much was it you got that time? When Cheltenham was on that time.

JIM. Two hundred and twenty.

JACK. Two hundred and twenty pounds, Valerie, in like three days, now. Right?

JIM. Yeah but . . .

JACK. Yeah, I know, that'd be a bigger win. But he was planning for Cheltenham for weeks, Valerie, and . . . tinkering with his figures and his . . . you know. He'd be in here with the paper up on the counter there. Brendan? Before Cheltenham?

BRENDAN. Yeah.

JACK. Right? Now, but I'm more: Ah, sure, I'll have an old bet, like. Do you know that way? And that's what I do, and to tell you the truth I don't be too bothered. It's a bit of fun and that's what it should be. And so . . . I'm not going to listen to 'Do this and do that, and you'll be right.' Just to get a few bob. There's no fun in that and the principle of it, you know?

FINBAR. Ah, the principle of the thing is to win a few quid and don't be giving out.

JACK. Who's giving out? I'm not giving out. All I'm saying is that the way I go at it, the principle's not, the science. It's the luck, it's the something that's not the facts and figures of it.

FINBAR. Jaysus. And do you and Kenny get down on your knees and lash a few quick Hail Marys out before he stamps your docket or something?

JACK. Ah it's not like that. I'm not talking about that. For fuck's sake.

FINBAR. Anyway, what the hell are you talking about? You took Jimmy's tip today, and you won so what the hell are you talking about? (*To others.*) Ha?

JACK. Ah yeah but . . . now listen because . . .

The others are laughing, going 'ah' as though FINBAR *has caught* JACK *out.*

I'll tell yous. If you won't listen . . . Right? I don't have a system. And I do. I do lose a few bob every now and then. Right? So I take a little tip from Jim. And then that'll finance having a couple of bets over the next few weeks.

They laugh.

And I've been known to have one or two wins myself, as well yous know and don't forget. I have one or two.

BRENDAN. You do not. Go on out of that you chancer.

JACK. I do.

FINBAR. I'd say the last win you had was fucking Red Rum or someone.

JACK (*aside to* VALERIE). We do be only messing like this.

FINBAR. What would anyone like? Jim?

JIM. Eh, small one then, thanks, Finbar.

FINBAR. Jack? Small one? Pint? Bottle, is it? You on the bottles?

JACK. No the tap is . . . fucking . . .

FINBAR. Oh. Typical.

JACK. Ah, I'll have a small one, go on.

FINBAR. Good man. Valerie?

VALERIE. Oh no, I'm okay for the moment, thanks.

FINBAR. Are you sure? Top that up?

VALERIE. No I'm fine, honestly.

FINBAR. You're sure now?

VALERIE. No really, I'm fine.

FINBAR (*hands up*). Fair enough. We won't force you. Give us . . . eh, three small ones, Brendan. Good man. Here, are you having one?

BRENDAN (*working*). I'm debating whether to have one.

JACK. Ah, he'll have one. Go on Brendan. Who knows when the hell you'll see another drink off the Finbar fella, ha? Come on! Quick! He's all annoyed you're having one.

FINBAR (*to* VALERIE). Would you listen to him?

JACK. That fella'd peel a banana in his pocket.

JIM. Is that what it is?

They laugh.

FINBAR. First time I've been in here for ages, bringing nice company in and everything, getting this. Oh you'd have to watch the Jimmy fella. There's more going on there than he lets on. 'Is that what that is?'

BRENDAN *places the drinks on the bar.*

And look at this! Me buying the drinks like a feckin eejit. Ah it's not right. What do you think Valerie?

VALERIE. Oh it's terrible.

FINBAR. Oh, it's desperate. (*He hands* BRENDAN *a twenty pound note.*) There you go, Brendan. I wouldn't say you see too many twenties in here. With the boys, wouldn't be too often, I'd say. Cheers boys.

JACK (*to* BRENDAN). Check that. Cheers.

JIM. Good luck.

BRENDAN. Good luck now.

VALERIE. Cheers.

JACK. How did you put up with that fella showing you around?

VALERIE. Ah, he was a bit quieter today.

JACK. Well. You're seeing the real him now. And I bet you prefer the other one. We've never seen it. The quiet Finbar. This one comes out at night, you see.

VALERIE. Oh, well I was getting the history of the place and everything today.

JACK. 'The history of the place.' You were probably making it all up on the spot, were you?

FINBAR. Yeah, I was, yeah. That's why all them photographs are fake. I had them done years ago just to fool Valerie, tonight.

VALERIE (*going to the photographs*). Oh right. That's all around here, is it?

FINBAR (*going to the photographs*). That's the weir. When was that taken, Brendan?

BRENDAN. Eh, that's 1951.

FINBAR. 1951. The weir, the river, the weir em is to regulate the water for generating power for the area and for Carrick as well. (*To* BRENDAN.) That's your dad there.

BRENDAN. Yeah. I think your dad's in it too.

FINBAR. Oh he is! Valerie, look at this. That's Big Finbar now. And that's Brendan's father, Paddy Byrne. This was when the ESB opened it. Big thing around here, Brendan.

BRENDAN. Oh yeah.

VALERIE (*to* FINBAR). You look like your father. (*To* BRENDAN.) You don't.

FINBAR. He's like his mother. He's like the Mangans. Now . . . Who would you say that is there. In the shorts.

VALERIE. Is it you?

FINBAR. Would you go on? The big fucking head on that yoke! Excuse the language. That's Jack.

VALERIE. Oh my God! How old were you there, Jack?

JACK. Em. Oh I was about seven.

VALERIE. I wouldn't have said that was you.

FINBAR. You must be joking, you'd spot that big mutton head anywhere. The photographer nearly had to ask him to go home, there wasn't going to be room in the picture. Isn't that right Jack?

JACK. That's right, and your dad nearly climbing into the camera there.

FINBAR. He was a pillar of the community, Valerie. No one had anything against him. Except headers like your man there. (*Indicating* JACK.)

JACK. That's right, Finbar. And I'm just going in here to do something up against the pillar of the community now.

JACK *goes out door at back.*

FINBAR. Jays, he's a desperate fella, that one.

VALERIE. Where was this taken?

BRENDAN. That's the view of Carrick from our top field up there.

VALERIE. It's an amazing view.

FINBAR. Oh I'd say that's probably one of the best views all around here, wouldn't it be?

BRENDAN. Oh yeah I'd say so.

JIM. Oh yeah, it would be, yeah.

FINBAR. You get all the Germans trekking up here in the summer, Valerie. Up from the campsite.

VALERIE. Right.

FINBAR. They do come up. This'd be the scenic part of all around here, you know? Em. There's what's? There was stories all, the fairies be up there in that field. Isn't there a fort up there?

BRENDAN. There's a kind of a one.

VALERIE. A fairy fort?

FINBAR. The Germans do love all this.

BRENDAN. Well there's a . . . ring of trees, you know.

FINBAR. What's the story about the fairy road that . . . Who used to tell it?

BRENDAN. Ah, Jack'd tell you all them stories.

FINBAR. There's all this around here, Valerie, the area's steeped in old folklore, and that, you know.

BRENDAN. Jack'd know . . . the what the, you'd know a few, Jim.

JIM. Ah Jack'd tell you better than me.

FINBAR (*at photograph*). That's the abbey now.

h.

see more of it there now. What was there,
was that?

ck in oh, fifteen something, there was a
all came and met there for . . . like . . . eh.

used to be quite important back a few
.....red years ago, Valerie. This was like the capital of the,
the county, it would have been.

VALERIE. Right.

JACK *comes back in.*

FINBAR. Oh it's a very interesting place all, eh, Jack we were
just saying about the, what was the story with the fairy
road?

JACK. The fairy road? I go into the toilet for two minutes.
I can't leave yous alone for two minutes . . .

They laugh.

FINBAR. Ah I was telling Valerie about the fort and
everything. What was the story with the fairy road? Where
was it?

Short pause.

JACK. Are you really interested? All the babies.

FINBAR. Ah it's a bit of fun. Tell her. Where was it?

JACK (*to* FINBAR). You're going to regret me saying this now,
'cause you know whose house it was?

FINBAR. Whose?

JACK. It was Maura Nealon's house.

FINBAR (*self-chastising, remembering*). Oh . . . Jesus.

They laugh.

JACK. You see? That's as much cop as you have now.

FINBAR. I fucking forgot it was Maura.

JACK. These are only old stories, Valerie.

VALERIE. No. I'd like to hear it.

JACK. It's only an old cod, like.

FINBAR. You're not going to be scaring the woman.

JACK. Ah it's not scary.

VALERIE. I'm interested in it.

FINBAR. You hear all old shit around here, it doesn't mean anything.

BRENDAN. This is a good little story.

JACK. It's only short. It's just. Maura . . . Nealon used to come in here in the evening, sit over there at the fire. How old was she, Jim? When she died?

JIM. Oh Jays, she would have been nearly ninety.

JACK. But she was a grand, you know, spritely kind of a woman 'til the end. And had all her . . . She was on the ball, like, you know? And she swore that this happened. When she was only a girl. She lived in that house all her life. And she had older brothers and sisters. She was the youngest. And her mother, eh . . .

JIM. Bridie.

JACK. Bridie. She was a well-known woman in the area. A widow woman. She was a bit of a character. Bit of a practical joker and that, you know? And Maura would say that when she was young, she was, Bridie was, always doing things on the older kids, hiding their . . . clothes and all this, you know? And she'd tell them old fibs about what a certain, prospective boyfriend or girlfriend had said about them out on the road and this about coming courting or that. And she was always shouting from upstairs or this 'There's someone at the door.' She was always saying there's someone at the back door or there's someone coming up the path. You know. This. And there'd never be, anyone there. And people got used to her. That she liked her joke.

And Maura used to say that one Saturday evening back in about 1910 or 1911, the older ones were getting ready to go out for a dance or whatever was happening. And the mother,

Bridie, came down the stairs and said, 'Did no one get the door?'

And they were all, 'Oh here we go,' you know? But – Bridie came down and *opened* the door, and there was nobody there. And she didn't say anything, And she wasn't making a big thing out of it, you know? And Maura said, she was only young, but she knew there was something wrong. She wasn't cracking the jokes. And later on, when the others were all out, it was just her and her mother sitting at the fire. And her mother was very quiet. Normally she'd send Maura up to bed, early enough, like. But Maura said she remembered this night because Bridie didn't send her up. She wanted someone with her, you see. And in those days, Valerie, as you know, there was no electricity out here.

And there's no dark like a winter night in the country. And there was a wind like this one tonight, howling and whistling in off the sea. You hear it under the door and it's like someone singing. Singing in under the door at you. It was this type of night now. Am I setting the scene for you?

They laugh.

Finbar's looking a bit edgy. You want to finish that small one, I think.

FINBAR. Don't mind my small one. You're making very heavy weather of this yarn, Jack.

JACK. Ah now, you have to enjoy it. You have to relish the details of something like this, ha?

They laugh.

So there they were, sitting there, and Bridie was staring into the fire, a bit quiet. And smiling now and again at Maura. But Maura said she could see a bit of wet in her eyes. And then there was a soft knocking at the door. Someone. At the front door. And Bridie never moved. And Maura said, 'Will I get the door, Mammy?' And Bridie said, 'No, sure, it's only someone playing a joke on us, don't mind them.' So they sat there, and there was no more knocking for a while. And, em, in those days, there was no kitchen. Where the extension is, Valerie, that was the back door and only a little

latch on it, you know? And that's where the next knocking
was. Very soft, Maura said, and very low down the door.
Not like where you'd expect a grown man or a woman to be
knocking, up here, you know? And again Bridie was saying,
ah, it's only someone having a joke, they'll go away.
And then it was at the window. Maura couldn't see anything
out in the night, and her mother wouldn't let her go over.
And then it stopped. But when it was late and the fire went
down, Bridie wouldn't get up to get more turf for the fire.
Because it was out in the shed. So they just sat there until
the others came back, well after midnight.

VALERIE. What was it?

JACK. Well Maura said her mother never told the others, and
one day when it was only the two of them there, a priest
came and blessed the doors and the windows. And there
was no more knocking then. And it was only years later that
Maura heard from one of the older people in the area that
the house had been built on what they call a fairy road. Like
it wasn't a road, but it was a . . .

JIM. It was like a row of things.

JACK. Yeah, like a . . . From the fort up in Brendan's top field
there, then the old well, and the abbey further down, and
into the cove where the little pebbly beach is, there. And the
. . . legend would be that the fairies would come down that
way to bathe, you see. And Maura Nealon's house was built
on what you'd call . . . that . . . road.

VALERIE. And they wanted to come through.

JACK. Well that'd be the idea. But Maura never heard the
knocking again except on one time in the fifties when the
weir was going up. There was a bit of knocking then she
said. And fierce load of dead birds all in the hedge and all
this, but that was it. That's the story.

FINBAR. You're not bothered by that, are you Valerie? 'Cause
it's only old cod, you know? You hear all these around, up
and down the country.

VALERIE. Well. I think there's probably something in them.
No, I do.

JACK. Ah, there . . . might be alright. But . . . it doesn't hurt. A bit of an old story, like. But I'll tell you what, it'd give you a thirst, like. You know? What'll yous have?

They laugh.

Valerie, top that up.

VALERIE. Em . . .

JACK. Go on.

FINBAR. Ah she will. Brendan.

BRENDAN *puts a clean tumbler on the bar.*

VALERIE. This glass is fine.

FINBAR. Oh, country ways! Good girl.

They laugh. BRENDAN *pours wine.*

JACK. Finbar. Pint?

FINBAR. Ah. Pint. Why not, says you, ha?

JACK. Jim?

JIM. Ah.

JACK. Two pints and one of these please, Brendan.

BRENDAN. Two pints.

Pause. BRENDAN *works.*

FINBAR. Yep. Oh yeah.

JACK. Are you debating to have one yourself?

BRENDAN. I'm debating.

FINBAR. Who's winning?

BRENDAN. Ah, it's a draw. I'm going to have a glass.

FINBAR. Good man. Have two, ha?

They laugh. JACK *produces cigarettes.*

JACK. Valerie?

VALERIE. Eh, I will, thanks.

FINBAR (*pleasantly surprised*). Oh! Good girl.

JACK. Finbar?

FINBAR. No I won't thanks Jack. Haven't had one of them fellas now, eighteen years this November.

JACK. Eighteen years, ha?

JACK *offers the pack to* BRENDAN *and* JIM *who both take one.*

FINBAR. Eighteen years. Not since I made the move. (*To* VALERIE.) Down to . . . Carrick.

JACK. I remember this. (*Lighting cigarettes.*) Jays, you don't look any better for it, ha?

They laugh.

FINBAR. Oh yeah? We'll see who'd look the better after a round or two of the fisty footwork ha? And you with the lungs hanging out your back.

JACK. Jaysus. An auldfella like me. Ten or more years between us and you wanting to give me a few digs. Business . . . killer instinct, is it?

FINBAR (*winks at* VALERIE). That's an eye for the gap. Exploit the weakness.

JACK. The weakness, yeah? Because talking of the fairy road. Didn't you have a little run in with the fairies or who was it, that time before you went?

FINBAR. Ah, now . . . Jaysus.

JACK. Because you were very brave that time, weren't you?

FINBAR. Ah Jack, for fuck's sake.

JACK. Ah come on now. You were great that time.

FINBAR. You're a bollocks.

JACK. Well, you. You know, talking of the fairies, now you know?

FINBAR. It wasn't the fairies. It was the . . . Walsh young one having us all on. It was only a cod, sure.

JIM. She's in America now. Niamh Walsh.

BRENDAN. It was Niamh that time, yeah?

FINBAR. Ah she was a header. Looking for attention.

VALERIE. What happened?

JACK. This was the brave fella.

FINBAR. Ah stop. It was nothing.

JACK. This was a family lived up beside Big Finbar's place.
The Walshes.

FINBAR. Ah they were only blow-ins, he was a guard.

VALERIE. Blow-ins like me?

FINBAR. Ah no. You know what I . . . what I mean.

JACK. Jays, you'll be losing business with them kind of
remarks, ha? Valerie will agree with me there now.

They laugh.

FINBAR. Ah she knows what I mean. Valerie's very welcome.
She knows that, don't you?

JACK. Ah leave her alone, you're embarrassing everybody
now. Jaysus.

They laugh.

Tell her the story.

FINBAR. Ah Janey. Sure you have her in a haunted house
already! She won't be able to sleep.

VALERIE. No. I'd like to hear it.

FINBAR. It's not even a real one.

JACK. Ah, she wants to hear one, don't be moaning and tell
her, come on.

FINBAR. Tch. Just a crowd of headbangers is all it was. There
was a house out near where we were on the other side of the
Knock there. It would have been the nearest place to us,
Valerie, about a quarter mile down the road. And the old lad
Finnerty, lived on his own down there, and his family got
him into a nursing home out by them down in Westport.
And the people who moved in were the Walshes, and your
man was a sergeant in the guards, stationed in Carrick. And,
like he was fifty-odd and still only a sergeant, so, like, he
was no Sherlock Holmes. You know?

They laugh.

He wasn't 'Walsh of the Yard' or anything like that. And
they moved in. He had three daughters who were teenagers,

and a youngfella who was married back near Longford there.
So the . . . daughters were with him and the missus. And I
knew them a little bit because that was the year Big Finbar
died, God rest him, and they arrived about the time of the
funeral so . . . you know, I met them, then. And I was living
on my own because me and Big Finbar were the only two in
it at that time. So I was the bachelor boy, and a gaggle of
young ones after moving in next door. Yo ho! You know?

They laugh.

And around that time I would have been wondering what to
do, Valerie, do you know? Whether to sell it on or farm it
or, you know. I was twenty-two, twenty-three, you know?
And it was, it would have been around eleven or twelve
o'clock this night and there was a knock at the door and it
was Mrs Walsh. And she was all upset and asking me if I
could come in, she didn't know what to do. The husband
was at work, out on a call, and she didn't know anyone in
the area, and there was a bit of trouble. So 'What kind of
trouble?' I says. And she says she was after getting a phone
call from the young one, Niamh, and she was after doing
the Luigi board, or what do you call it?

VALERIE. Ouija board.

FINBAR. Ouija board.

JACK. 'Luigi board!' She was down there in the chipper in
Carrick, was she, Finbar?

FINBAR. Ah fuck off. I meant the Ouija board. You know
what I meant. She was after being down in . . .

JACK. 'The Luigi board.'

FINBAR. She was after, come on now, she was after being
down in a friend of hers' house or this. And they were after
doing the . . . Ouija board. And she phoned her mother to
come and collect her. They said they were after getting a
spirit or this, you know, and she was scared, saying it was
after her.

And I obviously just thought, this was a load of bollocks,
you know? If you'll . . . excuse the language, Valerie. But
here was the mother saying she'd gone and picked her up.

I mean, like, sorry, but I thought it was all a bit mad. But on the way back they'd seen something, like the mother had seen it as well. Like a dog on the road, running with the car and running after it. Like there's dogs all around here, Valerie, you know? The farmers have them. There was a big dog up there, Jack, that Willie McDermott had that time.

JACK. Oh Jaysus, yeah, it was like a, if you saw it from the distance, you'd think it was a little horse. It was huge.

JIM. Saxon.

FINBAR. That was it. Saxon.

JIM. It was an Irish Wolfhound. He got it off a fella in the north.

FINBAR. Yeah it was huge. You'd be used to seeing dogs all around the place. All kinds, but they'd be tame, like. Their bark'd be worse than their bite. So I wasn't too . . . taken with this story. But she wanted me to come down to the house, because when they'd got back to the house, the young one, Niamh was going hysterical saying there was something on the stairs. Like, no one else could see it. But she could. And it was a, a woman, looking at her. And Mrs Walsh didn't know what to do. They couldn't contact the hubbie, and would I come down? I mean, what made her think there was anything I could do, I don't know. But she was panicking, you know . . . So I got in the car and we went down. And Jesus, now, I've never seen the like of it. The young one was in . . . bits. They had a blanket around her and she was as white, now as . . . (*Points to* JACK's *shirt.*) as white as that. Well whiter, because that's probably filthy.

JACK. Ha ha.

FINBAR. But I'm not messing. And she wouldn't come out of the living room. Because she said there was a woman on the stairs. And I said, what's the woman doing? And she said, 'She's just looking at me.' She was terrified. Now I didn't know whether she was after taking drugs or drink or what she was after doing. So I says to phone for Dr Joe in Carrick. This is Joe Dillon, Valerie, you'd see him in the town, he still has his surgery there beside the Spar. Very nice fella. And I got through to him, and he was on his way, and the Niamh one was shouting at me to close the living-room door. Because I was out in the hall where the phone was, and she could see the woman looking at her over the bannister. Like she was that bad, now. So Mrs Walsh phoned Father Donal, got him out of bed. And fair dues, like, he came down and sort of blessed the place a little bit. Like he'd be more Vatican two. There wouldn't be much of all the demons or that kind of carry-on with him.

JACK. Jaysus, sure, he'd collapse. He's like that. (*Holds up little finger.*) Him and a demon . . .

They laugh.

FINBAR. But Dr Joe gave her a sedative and off she went then, you know. And we all had a little drink, and poor Mrs Walsh was understandably, very, you know, shaken and everything. But Father Donal told her not to mind the Ouija, and it was only an old cod. And it was Niamh's imagination and all this. And then the phone rang, right? And it was the youngfella, the brother who was married back in Longford. And he was all, that his baby was crying and he had it out of the cot and he was standing at the window and there was all this commotion next door. Cars in the drive and all. That an aul one who lived next door who used to mind Niamh and the other sisters when they were young and all this, who was bedridden had been found dead at the bottom of the stairs. She fallen down, and they found her. And alright, whatever, coincidence. But . . . eh, that night, at home, I was sitting at the fire having a last fag before the sack, and, Jack'd know the house, the stairs come down into the, the main room. And I had my back to it. To the stairs. And it's stupid now, but at the time I couldn't turn around. I couldn't get up to go to bed. Because I thought there was something on the stairs. (*Low laugh.*)

And I just sat there, looking at an empty fireplace. And I sat there until it got bright. I was like a boy, you know? I wouldn't move in case something saw me. You know that way. I wouldn't even light another fag. Like I was dying for one, and I wouldn't . . . mad. But when it was bright then, I was grand, you know? Obviously there was nothing there and everything, but that was the last fag I ever had. (*Short pause.*) They moved away though, then, after that, the Walshes. (*Pause.*) Yep.

VALERIE. And that was when you moved. Down to Carrick.

FINBAR. Yeah. (*Nods slowly.*) Maybe that . . . had something to do with it. I don't know.

VALERIE. Mm.

JACK. Moving down into the lights, yeah?

FINBAR. Mmm. Might be. Might be, alright. Didn't want the loneliness maybe, you know? (*Pause.*) Yous all think I'm a loolah now.

They laugh.

Ha? I'm the header says you, ha? I'm going to powder my nose I think.

FINBAR *goes out door, back.*

JACK (*calling after him*). Sure, we knew you were a headbanger. Knew that all along.

They laugh. Pause.

Yeah.

VALERIE. I'd imagine though, it can get very quiet.

JACK. Oh it can, yeah. Ah, you get used to it. Brendan.

BRENDAN. Ah yeah you don't think about it.

JACK. Me and Brendan are the fellas on our own. Jim has the mammy to look after, but we're, you know, you can come in here in the evenings. During the day you'd be working. You know, there's company all around. Bit of a community all spread around the place, like.

JIM. You can put the radio on.

Pause.

JACK. Have you got any plans or that, for . . . here?

VALERIE. Not really, I'm just going to try and have some . . .

JACK. Peace and quiet.

VALERIE. Mm.

JACK. Jaysus, you're in the right place, so, ha?

They laugh.

You're going to have a peace and quiet . . . over . . . load. Oh yeah.

BRENDAN. Sure, you can always stick the head in here. Or Jack, or me or whatever, be able to sort you out for anything.

VALERIE. Thanks. I should be okay.

JACK. You're only ten minutes up the road. And Jaysus, by the looks of things you'll have a job keeping Finbar away, ha?

VALERIE. Ah he's a dote.

JACK. Jays, I've never heard him called that before, ha? Lots of other things, never that though.

FINBAR *comes back.*

FINBAR. What have you fecking heard? What are you talking about this time, Mullen, ha? About how twenty Germans were poisoned by the drink in here, last summer. (*Winks at* BRENDAN.) Ha?

JACK. No, I'd say the Arms is the place where that kind of carry-on happens. You'd get a pint in there, now, I believe, that'd put you on your back for a fortnight.

FINBAR. Don't mind them, Valerie, they're only jealous.

VALERIE. That's probably what it is, alright.

FINBAR. You see now? At least there's one person on my side.

JACK. Yeah, right. She's only sticking up for you to make sure she gets a lift after you scaring the living daylights out of her with your insistence on spooky stories.

FINBAR. Go on. It's only headers like me get a fright like that, ha? Fecking loolahs.

They laugh. JIM *counts some money.*

JIM. Does eh . . . Is anybody?

JACK. Ah no, Jim, I'm grand, you look after yourself.

JIM. Are you sure? Valerie?

VALERIE. I'll get you one.

FINBAR. Ah no Valerie, you're . . .

JACK. No, you're alright.

FINBAR. You're the guest. You're the guest.

JIM. Will you have a small one, Finbar?

FINBAR. Eh no, Jim. Thanks very much, I'm fine for the moment, finish this pint.

BRENDAN. Small one Jim? (*Pouring whiskey*.)

JIM. Thanks Brendan. I'll eh, I'll just lash a bit of turf in that, will I?

FINBAR. Good man, Jim.

BRENDAN *gives* JIM *his drink.* JIM *leaves money on the bar and goes to the fireplace, leaving his drink on the mantel.*

JACK. Keep the chill out, ha?

FINBAR. This is it.

FINBAR *looks at his watch.*

VALERIE. Do you want to?

FINBAR. Ah, no, no, no. I'm just watching the time. We've a wedding tomorrow.

VALERIE. Would you be . . . directly . . . working in the hotel?

JACK. Saves him paying someone's wages.

FINBAR. Sure that's how I have it, boy. (*He winks at* VALERIE.)

JACK. We know.

FINBAR. No there's certain things I do myself on a big day. One of the first things I ever learned in the business. The importance of good stock.

VALERIE. Soup stock?

FINBAR. For the soup. For the gravy, for the sauces, ah, you use it all over the place. And it's just a little thing I do. A little ritual. In the morning, I help do the stock. What do we have from yesterday and so on. A little mad thing I do, but there you are.

VALERIE. I think that's lovely.

FINBAR. Ah, it's a little thing I do. Little superstition. These'll tell you. I'm famous for it.

JACK. It's a gimmick.

BRENDAN. Who's geting married, Finbar?

FINBAR. Do you know Nuala Donnelly? 'Nu' they call her. She used to work for me in the Arms. Declan Donnelly's girl. Gas young one.

BRENDAN. Oh yeah.

FINBAR. You used to be pals with Declan, Jim.

JIM. Poor Declan. Be dead ten years in July. God rest him. Lovely fella.

FINBAR. She's a gas young one, the daughter. 'Nu' they call her. 'Call me Nu,' she says, the first day she was working for me. Not afraid to speak up for herself or anything. Used to tell us who was having affairs and all this. She was a chambermaid, you see. She knew the couples who were being all illicit because she'd go in to do the room in the morning and the bed would be already made. The woman in the affair would have done it out of guilt, you see. Cover it all up, for herself as much as for anyone else. She's a mad young one.

VALERIE. Would you get many people using the hotel like that?

FINBAR. Not at all. I wouldn't say so. But Nuala just, you know, she's a gabber and a talker.

JIM (*at stove*). Who's she getting married to, Finbar?

FINBAR. Oh Jesus, some fella from out the country. He must be in his forties. Shame, a young one getting hitched to an auld fell like that. He must have plenty of money. (*To* VALERIE, *indicating* JACK.) Be like getting married to that. He's a nice stash hidden away in that little garage, I'll tell you. Hoping to trap some little thing with it. Isn't that right, Jack?

JACK. That's my plan.

FINBAR. But you want to be careful of the old lads living on
their own. They've a big pot of stew constantly on the heat,
and they just keep throwing a few bits of scraps in it every
couple of days. And they'd survive on that, don't you Jack?
That'd do you?

JACK. It's a feast every day.

FINBAR. Aw. Dreadful fellas. And then they manage to get a
girl and the dust'd be like that on everything. And your
man'd be after living in two rooms all his life, and the poor
young one would have to get in and clean it all out. Thirty
years of old newspapers and cheap thrillers, all lying there
in the damp since their mammies died and that was the last
bit of cleaning went on in the place. That right Jack?

JACK. That's us to a tee.

BRENDAN. Jaysus, speak for yourself, ha?

FINBAR. Oh, they'd be desperate men. Changing the sheets in
the bed every Christmas. And there'd be soot all over
everything, and bits of rasher, and egg and pudding on the
floor.

VALERIE. The poor girl.

JACK. Poor girl is right. So the least I can do is make sure her
reception, in the Arms, is a little memory for her to have in
the future, in the cold nights. Cheers.

They have all enjoyed this.

You've a terrible warped mind, do you know that?

FINBAR (*winks at* VALERIE). Sure I'm only telling like it is,
ha?

JIM. Nuala getting married. You don't feel the time.

FINBAR. No.

JIM. Mmm. I remember, oh, it must have been twenty or more
years ago, doing a job with him. Declan. Talking about what
we were saying earlier. The priest over in Glen was looking
for a couple of lads to do a bit of work. And he was down in
Carrick in the Arms. He'd, come over, from Glen, you
know? Which was an odd thing anyway. Like what was he
doing coming all the way over just to get a couple of young

fellas? But Declan, Donnelly, got put on to him. There was
a few quid and he knocked up to me and we were to go over
to the church in Glen the following day. And I remember I
was dying with the 'flu and I had a terrible high
temperature. The mother was telling me to stay in the leaba.
Burn it off. But like it was a couple of quid on the QT so I
told Declan yeah, I'd do it tomorrow. No problem.

And then the next day it was lashing rain. I'll never forget
it. He called for me in his dad's car. The smell of sheep in it
like you wouldn't believe. God it would kill you. He used to
put them in the car, chauffeur them around, you know?

Smiles.

And we drove over to Glen. And the priest took us into the
sacristy, and the job, of all things was to dig a grave in the
yard. That day was the removal of the remains and they
needed the grave for the morning. And fair dues, like,
Declan said it to him. Was there no one else around the
place could have done it? And the priest got a bit cagey and
he was saying something about the local boys being busy
with a game of Gaa, or something. And the rain was pelting
down and he gave us leggings and wellies and the whole bit
they had there and a couple of shovels.

And then he put up his umbrella all annoyed, like, and he
brought us out, over to a grave under a tree. It was a family
one and there were two down in it already, the mother and
the father and this was going to be for the boy. Well he was
a man, like, a middle-aged fella. But there was two in it so
we weren't going to have to go down for miles, like. So he
went off to do his business and get ready, and me and
Declan got stuck in. And with the rain and all, I was dying
with the 'flu. My arms were sore and then my legs got sore.
And then my neck got sore. And I was boiling. But we got
down two, two-and-a-half foot and we took a break. We got
in Declan's car and he pulled out a bottle of poitin and a
few sambos. I couldn't eat but I took a good belt of the
bottle, like. Knocked me into some sort of shape. And we
just sat there for a while, listening to the radio, and the rain
coming down, and then we got out and got stuck in again.
Having a little swig every half hour or so, keeping it going.

And we saw the hearse arrive then. And the mad thing was, there was only two or three other fellas there for the service. Of course the removal is only a short thing mostly, but to have no one there, and for a man who's not an old man, it was funny, you know?

And then that was over and the priest came out to us. We were nearly finished. And he just cleared us for the funeral in the morning, and then he went off. So me and Declan were the only two there, then. (*Short pause.*) And your man was laid out in the church. And Declan went off to get a tarp to stretch over . . . the . . . grave, and I put a big lump of a door over it. And I was just waiting on Declan and having the last drop, under the tree and thinking we might stick the head in somewhere for a quick pint on the way back. You know?

And then I saw this, fella, come out of the church and he walked straight over to me. He was in a suit so I reckoned he was paying his respects or whatever. And over he comes, through the gravestones. And he was looking around him a bit, like he didn't know the place. And he stood beside me, under the tree, looking at the grave. I didn't know what to say, you know? And he goes, 'Is this for so and so?' I forget the name. And I go, 'That's right, yeah.' And he says, 'That's the wrong grave.' And I'm like, 'No. This is where the priest said, like.' And he looked at me, breathing hard through his nose. Like he was holding his temper. And he goes, 'Come on, I'll show you.' And he walks off.

And I was all like 'fuck this' you know? And I was cursing Declan, waiting for him to come back. And your man turns around, you know, 'Come on, it's over here.' I just, he was a loolah, you know? And I was nearly climbimg into the grave myself, with the tiredness. And I was sick. So I followed him just to get it over with. And he stopped at a grave. Like a new enough one. A white one with a picture of a little girl on it.

And he says, 'It's this one here.' And I just went, 'Okay, right you are Mister, I'll have it done, no problem. See you now.' And he . . . sort of touched the gravestone and he went

off, back into the church. I was breathing a few sighs of
relief I'll tell you. And Declan came back with the tarp and
I said, 'Did you see your man?' And he didn't know what
I was talking about. So I told him and all this, and we just
kind of had a bit of a laugh at it. And we just got out of
there. Stopped in the Green Man on the way back for a few
pints and that night my fever broke. But I was knackered.
The mother wouldn't let me go to the burial. Declan did it
on his own I think. But I was laid up for a couple of days.
And one day the mother brought me in the paper and on the
obituaries, there was a picture of your man whose grave
we'd dug. And you know what I'm going to say. It was the
spit of your man I'd met in the graveyard. So I thought first
it was a brother or a relative or someone, I'd met.

And I forgot about it a bit and didn't think about it for ages
until one night Declan told me he'd found out why the
priest from Glen was looking for a couple of Carrick fellas,
for the job. The fella who'd died had had a bit of a
reputation for em . . . being a pervert. And Jesus, when I
heard that, you know? If it was him. And he wanted to go
down in the grave with the . . . little girl. Even after they
were gone. It didn't bear . . . thinking about. It came back
when you said about Declan's girl. Yeah.

Pause.

FINBAR. Jaysus, Jim. That's a terrible story, to be telling.

JIM. Well, you know. And we'd been having the few little
drinks. From Dick Lenihan's batch, you know?

JACK. Oh Jesus. Firewater. Sure that'd put a hole in the glass,
let alone give you hallucinations.

A little laugh.

Pause.

VALERIE. Do you think it was a, an hallucination Jim?

JIM. God, I don't know. I was flying like, but it was a right
fluke him showing me where he wanted to be buried and me
knowing nothing about him like.

VALERIE. Mm. (*Nods.*)

FINBAR. Are you alright, Valerie? (*Little laugh.*) You look a bit peaky there.

VALERIE. No, I'm fine. Just, actually, is the ladies out this way?

BRENDAN. Ah. (*Short pause.*) Jays, I'll tell you what, Valerie, this is very embarrassing but the ladies is busted. And with the . . .

JACK *laughs.* BRENDAN *chuckles a little.*

I'm getting it fixed for the Germans like, but I haven't done it yet.

FINBAR. Ah, you're a terrible man, Brendan.

BRENDAN. No, I'll bring you in the house, come on.

VALERIE. Are you sure?

BRENDAN. Aw yeah, yeah, no problem.

JACK. Don't worry Valerie, if you're not back in ten minutes we'll come and get you, okay?

BRENDAN. Jaysus. Give it a rest. Come on Valerie, I'll put the lights on for you. Out this way.

FINBAR. Bye now.

VALERIE. Bye.

BRENDAN, *a little awkwardly, shepherds* VALERIE *out the back.*

Pause.

JACK. Yep.

Short pause.

FINBAR (*to* JIM). Jaysus. That's some fucking story. To be telling a girl, like. Perverts out in the country. For fuck's sake.

Short pause.

JACK. Like your story had nothing in it, ha?

FINBAR. Ah that was only old headers in it.

JACK. But you brought the whole thing up. With the fairies. The fairies! She's in that house.

FINBAR. I forgot it was that house. I forgot it was Maura
Nealon. It was an honest mistake.

JACK. Honest mistake.

FINBAR. What?

JACK. Don't be giving it that old cod now.

FINBAR. What do you mean?

JACK. With bringing her around and all.

FINBAR. What about it?

JACK. Bringing her up the Head and all.

Short pause. FINBAR *looks at* JIM *and back at* JACK.

FINBAR.Yeah?

JACK. So don't be giving it the old cod now.

FINBAR. What cod, Jack? (*Pause.*) I'm asking you. (*Short
pause.*) What?

JIM. Ah boys, we have a small one. Come on now.

FINBAR. Hang on a minute, Jim. What?

JACK. Well you get me to tell a story about the house she's in.

FINBAR. I didn't *know* that though. I told you that.

JACK. Whatever. And then you tell the story about the Walsh
girl.

FINBAR. Sure it was you told me to say that.

JACK. What?

FINBAR. Talking about the fags and giving up the fags and all
that. When you offered them that time.

JACK. Would you cop on? 'Ghosts' and 'Giving up the fags.'

FINBAR. Okay. I'm sorry. What? I regret the stories, then. I
don't think we should have any more of them. But that's
what I'm saying, like.

JIM. I didn't think. I just said it. With, Declan Donnelly and
that. It just, you know . . .

FINBAR. Ah no no no. Jim. We're not blaming anybody. I
regret it now. And let's not have any more of them, and
that's all.

JACK. Oh you regret it now?

FINBAR. Yeah.

JACK. It's not part of the tour.

FINBAR. Ah now, come on.

JACK. Bit of local colour.

FINBAR. No. Jack.

JACK. Just don't berate Jim for telling a story after you telling one yourself.

FINBAR. I apologise, if that's what I did. Sorry Jim. Now, I'll say that. But stop with this . . . tour guide thing. That's not fair. The woman's moved out here on her own. For some reason. There's something obviously going on . . . in her life. I'm just trying to make it easier for her. Give her a welcome, for fuck's sake. So don't . . . be implying anything else. I don't like it. (*Pause.*) I've apologised to Jim. And I'm saying no more stories. (*Short pause.*) Sure I'm married! I mean really. Yous are the single boys. (*Short pause. Warm.*) Sure I can't remember the last time I saw a suit on you.

Pause.

JACK. Oh now it's me?

JIM. Ah now boys, come on. That's enough. That's enough of that.

JACK. You think I have intentions, is it?

FINBAR. I don't know. You're entitled.

JACK. I do often wear a suit. Don't come in here for the first time in God knows, thinking we're fucking hicks. 'Cause you're from round here.

Pause.

FINBAR. Nobody's saying that. You've got the wrong idea, Jack. And it's not worth falling out over. Now, I'll buy you a drink. And that'll be the fucking end of it now. Alright?

JACK. You will not buy me a fucking drink. (*Short pause.*) I'll buy *you* one, and *that'll* be the end of it.

JACK *extends his hand. They shake.*

JIM. That's more like it, men. That's more like it, ha?

JACK *goes in behind the bar.*

JACK. What'll yous have?

FINBAR (*offering hand to* JIM). Sorry Jim.

JIM. Ah no no no. Stop. (*Shaking hands.*) It's forgotten.

JACK. Finbar.

FINBAR. Ah. I think I'll just have a glass, Jack, I think.

JACK. Ah, you'll have a small one with that.

FINBAR. Jays, you'll fucking kill me now, ha? I think he's trying to kill me Jim, is he?

JIM. Oh now.

JACK. Jim?

JIM. Small one, Jack, thanks.

JACK. You'll have a little pint with that I think.

JIM. Go on, ha?

FINBAR. Ah good man. (*Pause.*) Jays. That was a hot one there for a minute, ha?

JACK. We'll say no more about it. We might tell a few jokes when she comes back.

They laugh.

FINBAR. Jays. This is it. How's the mammy, Jim?

JIM. Ah, do you know what it is? She's just old. And everything's going on her.

FINBAR. Ah Jaysus, ha? I'll have to get up and see her.

JACK. I was saying that earlier. It'd be the time, you think, Jim.

JIM. Ah.

FINBAR. She does be alright on her own, with coming out for an old jar or that.

JIM. Oh don't mind her. She's well able to tell you what's what. The only thing would be the eyes. But she's the one.

I'm always mixing up the tablets. She knows exactly what she's supposed to be taking when. So. But we have the telly in that room. And she'll listen to that and drop off.

FINBAR. Well that's alright, isn't it.

JIM. Oh she's still . . . I'm taking her over to see her sister in the, in the order.

JACK. That's a closed order, Jim, yeah?

JIM. Yeah, you know. They don't talk and all that. But the sister is six years older than the mammy, now, you know, so . . .

FINBAR. Gas. She'll be alright for the drive?

JIM. Oh, she'll be knackered, she'll be out like a light when we get back.

FINBAR. Ah.

JIM. Ah yeah.

BRENDAN and VALERIE come back.

BRENDAN. So this was all the original. Before the house.

VALERIE. Right.

FINBAR. There you are, we thought we were going to have to send out a search party.

VALERIE. I was having a good nosy around.

FINBAR. Wasn't too much of a state, no?

VALERIE. Tidier than I normally am.

JACK. That's he had the sisters over today. That's all that is.

FINBAR. I saw them having their lunch in my place today.

BRENDAN. Don't be talking.

FINBAR (*gingerly*). Oh . . . back off there. Sensitive area. Eh, Valerie, darling, I don't want you to be stranded here with me now if I'm keeping you.

BRENDAN. Sure we can look after her.

FINBAR. Ah no, I'm grand for a while yet.

VALERIE. I, em. Hearing about. All these . . . you know, stories. It's . . .

FINBAR. Ah that's the end of them, now. We've had enough of
them old stories, they're only an old cod. We've just been
joking about it there when you were out. We'll all be, all be
witless, ha? We won't be able to sleep in our beds!

VALERIE. No, see, something happened to me. That just
hearing you talk about it tonight. It's important to me. That
I'm not . . . bananas.

I mean, I'm a fairly straight . . . down the line . . . person.
Working. I had a good job at DCU. I had gone back to work
after having my daughter, Niamh. My husband teaches,
engineering, at DCU. We had Niamh in 1988. And I went
back to work when she was five, when she started school.
And we'd leave her with Daniel's parents, my husband's
parents. His mother always picked her up from school. And
I'd collect her after work. And last year she, she was dying
to learn how to swim.

And the school had a thing. They'd take the class down to
the CRC in Clontarf on Wednesdays. She was learning very
well. No problem. Loved the water. She couldn't wait for
Wednesdays and swimming. Daniel used to take her to the
pool on Saturdays and everything.

But for such a bright, outgoing, happy girl she was a big em
. . . She had a problem sleeping at night. She was afraid of
the dark. She never wanted you to leave the room.

One of us would have to lie there with her until she went
off, and even when she did, she'd often have to come in and
sleep with us.

And I'd say to her, 'What's wrong, when you go to bed?'
But in the daytime, you know, she wouldn't care. Night-
time was a million miles away. And she wouldn't . . . think
about it. But at night . . . there were people at the window,
there were people in the attic, there was someone coming
up the stairs. There were children knocking, in the wall.
And there was always a man standing across the road who
she'd see. Like there was loads of things. The poor . . .
I wanted to bring her to the doctor, but Daniel said she'd
grow out of it. And we should be careful, just, about books
we got her, and what she saw on the telly and all of this.

But I mean, she used to even be scared that when she got up in the morning that Mammy and Daddy would have gone away and she'd be in the house on her own. That was one she told Daniel's mother. And all the furniture and carpets and everything would be gone. I mean, you know? So I told her after that, you know, we'd never, you know, it was ridiculous. And that if she was worried at all during the day to ring me, and I'd come and get her, and there was nothing to worry about. And she knew our number, she was very good at learning numbers off and everything. She knew ours and her Nana's and mine at work. She knew them all.

But then, in March, last year, the school had a, a sponsored swim, and the kids were going to swim a length of the pool. And I promised I was going to watch her. But I got . . . I was late, out of work, and I was only going to be in time to meet her afterwards, but em, when I got there . . . There was an ambulance and I thought, like, the pool is in the Central Remedial Clinic, so I thought like it was just somebody being dropped there. I didn't really pay any attention.

But when I got in, I saw that there was no one in the pool and one of the teachers was there with a group of kids. And she was crying and some of the children were crying. And this woman, another one of the mums came over and said there'd been an accident. And Niamh had hit her head in the pool and she'd been in the water and they'd been trying to resuscitate her. But she said she was going to be alright.

And I didn't believe it was happening. I thought it must have been someone else. And I went into, I was brought into, a room and Niamh was on a table. It was a table for table-tennis, and an ambulance man was giving her the . . . kiss of life.

She was in her bathing suit. And the ambulance man said he didn't think what he was doing was working. And he didn't know if she was alive. And he wrapped her in a towel and carried her out to the ambulance. And I got in the back with him. And they radioed on ahead, they were going to put her on a machine in Beaumont and try to revive her there. But the ambulance man knew, I think. She wasn't breathing, and he just knew, and he said if I wanted to say goodbye to her in the ambulance in case I didn't get a chance at the hospital.

And I gave her a little hug. She was freezing cold. And I told her Mammy loved her very much. She just looked asleep but her lips were gone blue and she was dead.

And it had happened so fast. Just a few minutes. And I don't think I have to tell you. How hard it was. Between me and Daniel, as well. It didn't seem real. At the funeral I just thought I could go and lift her out of the coffin and would be the end of all this.

I think Daniel was. I don't know if he actually, blamed me, there was nothing I could do. But he became very busy in his work. Just. Keeping himself . . . em. But I was, you know, I was more, just I didn't really know what I was doing. Just walking around, wanting to . . . Sitting in the house, with Daniel's mother, fussing around the place.

Just, months of this. Not really talking about it, like.

Pause.

But, and then one morning. I was in bed, Daniel had gone to work. I usually lay there for a few hours, trying to stay asleep, really. I suppose. And the phone rang. And I just left it. I wasn't going to get it. And it rang for a long time. Em, eventually it stopped, and I was dropping off again. But then it started ringing again, for a long time. So I thought it must have been Daniel trying to get me. Someone who knew I was there.

So I went down and answered it. And. The line was very faint. It was like a crossed line. There were voices, but I couldn't hear what they were saying. And then I heard Niamh. She said, 'Mammy?' And I . . . just said, you know, 'Yes.'

Short pause.

And she said . . . She wanted me to come and collect her. I mean, I wasn't sure whether this was a dream or her leaving us had been a dream. I just said, 'Where are you?'

And she said she thought she was at Nana's. In the bedroom. But Nana wasn't there. And she was scared. There were children knocking in the walls and the man was standing across the road, and he was looking up and he was going to cross the road. And would I come and get her?

And I said I would, of course I would. And I dropped the phone and I ran out to the car in just a teeshirt I slept in. And I drove to Daniel's mother's house. And I could hardly see, I was crying so much. I mean, I knew she wasn't going to be there. I knew she was gone. But to think wherever she was . . . that . . . And there was nothing I could do about it.

Daniel's mother got a doctor and I . . . slept for a day or two. But it was . . . Daniel felt that I . . . needed to face up to Niamh being gone. But I just thought that he should face up to what happened to me. He was insisting I get some treatment, and then . . . everything would be okay. But you know, what can help that, if she's out there? She still . . . she still needs me.

Pause.

JACK. You don't think it could have been a dream you were having, no?

Short pause.

VALERIE. I heard her.

Short pause.

FINBAR. Sure, you were after getting a terrible shock, Valerie. These things can happen. Your . . . brain is trying to deal with it, you know? (*Pause.*) Is your husband going to . . . come down?

VALERIE. I don't think so.

FINBAR. Ah, it'd be a terrible shame if you don't . . . if you didn't see . . . him because of something as, as, you know . . . that you don't even know what it was.

Short pause.

BRENDAN. She said she knew what it was.

FINBAR. But sure you can't just accept that, that you, you know . . . I mean . . . surely you, you have to look at the broader thing of it here.

JIM. It might have been a wrong number.

BRENDAN. What?

JIM. It could have been a wrong number or something wrong with the phone, you know? And you'd think you heard it. Something on the line.

BRENDAN. But you wouldn't hear someone's voice on the fucking thing, Jim.

JIM. Just it might have been something else.

JACK. Here, go easy, Brendan, Jim's only trying to talk about the fucking thing.

FINBAR. Ah lads.

JACK. Just take it easy.

VALERIE. Stop. I don't want . . . It's something that happened. And it's nice just to be here and . . . hear what you were saying. I know I'm not crazy.

Short pause.

FINBAR. Valerie, love, nobody's going to think that. But . . . just . . . no one knows about these things, sure, they're not real even. You hear all sorts of old cod, all around. But there's usually some kind of explanation for it. Sure, Jim said himself he was delirious with the 'flu that time. Jim.

JIM. I had a right temperature.

FINBAR. Maura . . . eh . . . Nealon, sure she was in here every night of the week. Brendan. About how much would she drink? Be honest now.

BRENDAN. How much did she drink?

JACK. Have a bit of respect, Finbar.

FINBAR. I'm trying to make a point, Jack. The woman was a drinker.

JACK. We're all drinkers.

FINBAR. But, come on. She was an alcoholic, Valerie. She used to have a bottle of whiskey put away before you knew where you were. Sure who wouldn't be hearing knocking after that?

JACK. Ah you're not being fair on her now. The woman's dead, she can't defend herself.

FINBAR. I'm not casting anything on her. If she came in that door right now, if she was alive, I'd be buying her drink, and more power to her, I'd hope she'd enjoy it. I'd be the first to buy her a drink. But I run a bar myself down in the Arms. And I know all about what a right few drinks'll do to you. She liked her drop is what I'm saying.

BRENDAN. What about you? And the Walshes?

FINBAR. Look. How many times do I have to say it? They were all a bunch of fucking headbangers!

Pause.

I got the wind put up me that night. Fair enough. But that's what these stories do. But I resent that now. What I went through that night. But I was only young. And that's over with, fucking headbangers.

Pause.

And after all that, I'm ignoring the bigger thing. I'm very sorry about your daughter, Valerie, I'm very sorry indeed.

JACK. Oh we all are. Of course we are. It's terrible.

Long pause.

FINBAR (*checks watch*). I'm going to have to go, I'm afraid. I don't want to, but . . .

VALERIE. Okay.

BRENDAN. Ah here, I'll leave her down.

FINBAR. But you might want to come on now, no?

VALERIE. Em.

BRENDAN. Ah, have another drink and relax for a little while.

VALERIE. Yeah, I think I'm going to hang on for another little while.

FINBAR. Are you going to go easy on the old stories?

JACK. Ah stop being an old woman. She'll be grand.

FINBAR. Alright?

JACK. She'll be grand.

JIM. Could I get a lift, Finbar?

FINBAR. Of course you can, Jim.

JACK. You're okay for Father Donal's car in the morning.

JIM (*counting money*). No problem. I'll be there about quarter to nine.

JACK. Grand, just, I've got to get out to Conor Boland.

JIM. Yeah. It's fine. Brendan, em . . .

BRENDAN. Naggin?

JIM. Please.

BRENDAN *puts a small bottle of whiskey in a plastic bag and gives it to* JIM. JIM *attempts to pay for it.* BRENDAN *discreetly waves him away.*

FINBAR. Yep.

JIM. Well. Valerie.

VALERIE. It was very nice to meet you.

JIM (*taking her hand*). I'm very sorry about what's happened to you. And I'm sure your girl is quite safe and comfortable wherever she is, and I'm going to say a little prayer for her, but I'm sure she doesn't need it. She's a saint. She's a little innocent. And that fella I saw in the churchyard that time was only the rotten poitin and the fever I had. Finbar's right. You enjoy your peace and quiet here now. And we'll see you again. You're very nice. Goodnight now.

VALERIE. Goodnight. Thanks Jim.

JIM. That's alright.

FINBAR. Valerie. (*He takes her hand.*)

VALERIE. Thanks for everything.

FINBAR. My pleasure, darling. And I'll call up to you now in the next day or two, and . . . (*Nods at her.*)

VALERIE. Fine.

FINBAR. And we'll make sure you're alright and you're settling in with us. You're very welcome.

He kisses her awkwardly on the cheek.

VALERIE. Thanks for everything, Finbar.

FINBAR. That's quite alright. Men.

JACK. Finbar.

FINBAR. I'll see you soon, I hope, Jack.

They shake hands.

Alright?

JACK. See you soon.

FINBAR. Brendan.

BRENDAN. Take it easy now, Finbar. Look after yourself.

FINBAR. I won't leave it so long next time.

BRENDAN. Okay.

JIM. Goodnight.

BRENDAN. Goodnight Jim.

VALERIE. See you soon.

JACK. See you in the morning.

JIM. Quarter to nine.

FINBAR. See yous now.

JIM *and* FINBAR *leave.*

JACK. There you are now.

BRENDAN. Mm.

JACK. I'm sorry for snapping. That time.

BRENDAN. Ah no. Sure. I was . . .

VALERIE. I think it was my fault.

JACK. Would you go on? Of course it wasn't your fault. You
know . . . It's all very well, us sitting around, fecking
around with these old stories. But then, for something
personal like that. That's happened to you. People are going
to deal with it, in different ways. Jim, was, you know . . .

BRENDAN. Yeah . . .

JACK. He didn't mean anything.

BRENDAN. He didn't really mean there was anything wrong with your phone, I don't think.

They laugh a little. Pause.

JACK. It's em . . . a terrible thing that happened. Do you ever get over something like that, I wonder? I don't mean the phone . . . call, you know.

VALERIE. I know. (*Pause.*) I don't know. (*Pause.*)

JACK. We're very sorry.

BRENDAN. Come on we sit near the stove. It's getting cold. We'll have a last one.

JACK. Good idea.

BRENDAN. Give us your glass, Valerie. Jack, you'll have a small one, for the road.

VALERIE. Can I get this?

JACK. Ah no no no.

BRENDAN. It's on the house now. Bar's officially closed. Go on.

JACK *and* VALERIE *move nearer the stove.*

JACK. You get yourself in there now. We'll be grand in a minute.

BRENDAN. I'm going to give you a little brandy, Valerie. This wine is freezing in the fridge.

JACK. Good man.

VALERIE. Oh lovely. Thanks.

JACK. Good girl. That's it now. (*To* BRENDAN.) Jim'll be in a bad way, all the same when the mammy goes, what do you think Brendan?

BRENDAN. Oh definitely. She's been very sick, Valerie, for years now. Fading fast, like, for years! She still spoils that boy rotten, ha? Though.

JACK. Oh definitely. Oh yeah.

BRENDAN *brings the drinks over.*

VALERIE. That's an awful lot.

BRENDAN. Ah it's not really.

JACK. There's no law says you have to drink it all, ha? Your man does put it back in the bottle.

BRENDAN. Would you ever fuck off?

JACK. I think we should drink this to you, sweetheart.

BRENDAN. Yes. To Valerie.

JACK. Hope it's all . . . (*Raises glass.*) In the end . . .

BRENDAN. Cheers.

VALERIE. Cheers.

They drink. JACK *considers* BRENDAN *for a moment.*

JACK. There's the boy, ha?

They smile.

VALERIE. You've no children, Jack, no?

JACK. No, darling, never married. But I do be telling this fella to be on the lookout. A youngfella like him. Not to end up like me.

VALERIE. Do you wish you had married?

JACK. Sure who'd have me? A cantankerous old fucker like me.

BRENDAN. Too right.

JACK. Yeah . . . It's a thing, you know? I do say it to Brendan. I'm down in the garage. And the fucking tin roof on the thing. On my own on that country road. You see it was bypassed by the main road into Carrick. And there's no . . . like in the summer the heat has the place like an oven, with the roof, or if it's not that, it's the rain pelting down on it like bricks, the noise of it. And there you'll be, the only car stopping in be someone that knows the area real well. Ah, you'd definitely feel it, like. But you know. I get down here for a pint and that. There's a lot to be said for the company. And the . . . you know, the . . . someone there. Oh yeah.

VALERIE. Did you never consider it? When you were young.

JACK. Oh sure. Yeah. Of course I did. Sure what the hell else does a youngfella be thinking about? You know?

And Brendan knows. I had a girl. A lovely girl back then.
We were courting for three, years, and em . . . 1963 to '66.
But she wanted to go up to Dublin, you know. She would
have felt that's what we should have done. And I don't
know why it was a thing with me that I . . . an irrational
fear, I suppose, that, kept me here. And I couldn't
understand why she wanted to be running off up to Dublin,
you know? And she did in the end, anyway, like. And she
was working up there waiting for me to come.

But with me it was a mad thing, that I thought it was a
thousand fucking miles away. Hated going up.

I went up a few times like. But . . . I was going up for . . .
you know . . . she had a room. A freezing, damp place. I
was a terrible fella. It became that that was the only thing
I was going for. I couldn't stand being away. I don't
know why. Ah, I'd be all excited about going up for the
physical . . . the freedom of it. But after a day and a night,
and I'd had my fill, we'd be walking in the park and I'd be
all catty and bored, and moochy.

Pause.

Breaking the poor girl's heart. Ah, you get older and look
back on why you did things, you see that a lot of the time,
there wasn't a reason. You do a lot of things out of pure
cussedness.

I stopped answering her letters. And I'd fucking dread one
coming to the house. And her in it wondering how I was and
was there something wrong with the post or this.

Pause.

I can't explain what carry on I was up to. I had just . . . left
her out. Being the big fella, me dad handing over the
business to me. Me swanning around. A man of substance.
And then I had the gall to feel resentful when she wrote and
said she was getting married to a fella.

Pause.

And I was all that it was her fault for going up in the first
place. Tss.

There was a delegation of people from all around here
going up to the wedding on a bus. And I was just one of the
crowd. Just one of the guests. In my suit, and the shoes
nearly polished off me. And a hangover like you wouldn't
believe. I'd been up 'til five or more, swilling this stuff,
looking at the fire. And we were all on the bus at nine. And
all the chat all around was why she hadn't come home to
get married. And me sick as a dog.

The smell of Brylcreem off all us culchies. Sitting in the
church in Phibsboro. All her lovely-looking nurse friends
and their guard boyfriends. She was marrying a guard. Huge
fella. Shoulders like a big gorilla. And they were coming
down the aisle after, and I caught her eye. And I gave her
the cheesiest little grin you've ever seen. A little grin that
was saying, 'Enjoy your big gorilla, 'cause the future's all
ahead of me.'

And she just looked at me like I was only another guest at
the wedding. And that was that. And the future *was* all
ahead of me. Years and years of it. I could feel it coming.
All those things you've got to face on your own. All by
yourself. And you bear it 'cause you're showing everybody
that you're a great fella altogether.

But I left the church like a little boy. And I walked away. I
couldn't go to the reception. I just kept walking. There was
a light rain. I just kept walking. And then I was in town. It
was a dark day. Like there was a roof on the city. And I
found myself in a little labyrinth of streets. With nothing
doing. And I ducked into a pub. Little dark place. Just one
or two others there. A businesslike barman. Like yourself
Brendan, ha?

Businesslike, dutiful. And I put a pint or two away. And a
small one or two. And I sat there, just looking down at the
dirty wooden bar. And the barman asked me if I was alright?
Simple little question. And I said I was. And he said he'd
make me a sandwich. And I said okay. And I nearly started
crying – because, you know, here was someone just . . . and
I watched him.

He took two big slices off a fresh loaf and buttered them carefully, spreading it all around. I'll never forget it. And then he sliced some cheese and cooked ham and an onion out of a jar, and put it all on a plate and sliced it down the middle. And, just someone doing this for me. And putting it down in front of me. 'Get that down you now,' he said. And then he folded up his newspaper and put on his jacket and went off on his break. And there was another barman then.

And I took this sandwich up and I could hardly swallow it, because of the lump in my throat. But I ate it all down because someone I didn't know had done this for me. Such a small thing. But a huge thing in my condition. It fortified me, like no meal I ever had in my life. And I went to the reception. And I was properly ashamed of myself. There was a humility I've tried to find since. But goodness wears off. And it just gets easier to be a contrary bollocks.

Down in the garage. Spinning small jobs out all day. Taking hours to fix a puncture. Stops you thinking about what might have been and what you should have done. It's like looking away. Like I did at that reception. You should only catch someone's eye for the right reason. And I'll tell you – there's not one morning I don't wake up with her name in the room. (*Pause.*)

And I do be at this fella. Don't I? (*Pause.*) Yep. (*Pause.*) I may be on my way now.

BRENDAN. Will you be okay in that wind?

JACK. Jaysus, I should be used to that road by now, says you, ha?

BRENDAN. I'll get you the torch.

JACK. Am I a moaner?

BRENDAN (*going*). There's well fucking worse, I'll tell you.

He exits.

JACK. Well. That wasn't a ghostly story. Anyway. At least, ha?

VALERIE. No.

JACK. We've had enough of them. (*Pause.*) We'll all be ghosts soon enough, says you, ha?

VALERIE. Mmm.

JACK. We'll all be sitting here. Sipping whiskey all night with Maura Nealon. (*Pause.*) Yeah. (*Short pause.*) This has been a strange little evening for me.

VALERIE (*a little laugh*). For me as well.

JACK. Fuck. We could do worse. It was lovely to meet you.

VALERIE. You too.

JACK. I didn't mean to go on there.

VALERIE. No, please . . .

JACK. Something about your company. Inspiring, ha? And this of course. (*Glass.*)

They smile.

I wonder if being out here in the country is the best place for you to . . . you know . . .

VALERIE. Why?

JACK. Ah. Girl like you. Hiding yourself away. Listening to old headers like us talking about the fairies. Having all your worst fears confirmed for you. Tuh. Ghosts and angels and all this? Fuck them. I won't have it. Because I won't see someone like you being upset by it. You've enough to . . . deal with, for fuck's sake. I am very, sorry, love, about what happened.

VALERIE. Thanks.

BRENDAN *comes in turning the torch on and off.*

BRENDAN. The batteries are a bit weak. Come on, I'll drop you.

JACK. Are you sure?

BRENDAN. Sure, I'm giving Valerie a lift.

VALERIE. Come with us.

JACK. Okay, then. Grand.

BRENDAN *is clearing glasses, going in behind the bar, tidying up.*

VALERIE. Do you want a hand, Brendan?

BRENDAN. Oh no! Stay where you are, I'll be finished in a sec.

JACK *takes his anorak, joking.*

JACK. Is this yours, Valerie?

VALERIE. Yeah right.

JACK *takes her jacket and holds it for her to put on.*

JACK. Come on.

VALERIE. Oh now. Very nice.

JACK. These are the touches, ha, Brendan?

BRENDAN. That's them.

JACK. Now.

VALERIE. Thanks.

JACK. Mmm. Have a last fag I think.

Taking cigarette packet.

Anyone else?

VALERIE. No, I won't thanks.

BRENDAN. No, I'm grand thanks, Jack.

JACK. Up early in the morning. Over to Conor Boland. He's over the other side of Carrick there. Has about fifteen fucking kids. Dirty bollocks.

BRENDAN *and* VALERIE *laugh.*

And you should see her. Built like a fucking tractor. The head on her.

BRENDAN. You're a terrible man.

JACK. I've had my moments.

BRENDAN *looks at* VALERIE *and shakes his head.*

VALERIE. Will you be in here again soon?

JACK. Ah I'm always in and out. Got to keep the place afloat at least, you know?

BRENDAN (*working*). Don't mind him now, Valerie. Him and the Jimmy fella'll be fierce scarce around here the next few weeks.

VALERIE. Why?

BRENDAN (*stops work and lights a cigarette*). All the Germans'll be coming and they love it in here.

VALERIE (*to* JACK). You don't like that?

JACK *makes a face.*

BRENDAN. He thinks they're too noisy.

JACK. See, you don't know what they do be saying or anything.

BRENDAN. Him and Jimmy be sitting there at the bar with big sour pusses on them. Giving out like a couple of old grannies.

JACK. Ah we're not that bad.

BRENDAN. You're like a pair of bloody auld ones, you should see them.

VALERIE. Where do you go instead?

JACK. Ah, place down in Carrick, the Pot.

BRENDAN (*derision*). 'The Pot'. There does be just as many of them down there don't be codding yourself.

JACK. Ah no, it doesn't seem as bad down there, now.

VALERIE. That's because this is your place.

JACK. Now. You've hit it on the head. You see, Brendan, Valerie's defending us. It's out of respect for this place.

BRENDAN. It is in my fucking barney respect! The two of yous leaving me standing behind that bar with my arms folded, picking my hole and not knowing what the hell is going on. And them playing all old sixties songs on their guitars. And they don't even know the words.

And nothing for me to do except pull a few pints and watch the shadow from the Knock moving along the floor, with the sun going down. I'm like some fucking mentler, I do be watching it! Watching it creeping up on the Germans. And they don't even notice it. I must be cracking up if that's my entertainment of an evening.

JACK. Ah don't be moaning. I'll tell you what. If Valerie's willing to come in and brave the Germans, then I'm sure me and Jim'll come in and keep yous company, how's that now?

BRENDAN. Oh you'll *grace* us with your ugly mushes, will you?

JACK. Don't push it, boy. Ah sure, Jaysus, what am I talking about? Sure you'll have Finbar in here sniffing around Valerie every night anyway.

VALERIE. Ah now stop.

They laugh a little.

JACK. He'll be like a fly on a big pile of shite, so he will. Jesus. That came out all wrong, didn't it?

BRENDAN. No Jack. That was perfect. As usual.

JACK. Couldn't have come out worse. Sorry about that.

VALERIE. Would you relax?

BRENDAN *is putting his jacket on.*

JACK. Sorry. Will you anyway?

VALERIE. What? Come in . . . with the . . . Germans?

JACK. Yeah.

VALERIE. Doesn't bother me.

JACK. Ah, I think that's the right attitude. You should stay with the company and the bright lights.

BRENDAN (*looking around*). Do you see my keys?

VALERIE *and* JACK *look around a little bit.*

VALERIE. Sure I might even learn some German.

JACK. Ah, I don't know. They're eh . . . Are they from Germany, Brendan?

BRENDAN. What?

JACK. The Germans. (*To* VALERIE.) We call them the Germans.

VALERIE *picks keys off the mantelpiece.*

VALERIE. Is this them?

BRENDAN. Yeah, thanks. Are we right?

They are moving towards the door.

JACK. Where are they from. Is it Denmark, or Norway? (*To* VALERIE.) It's somewhere like that.

JACK *goes out, followed by* VALERIE.

BRENDAN. Ah I don't know where the fuck they're from.

BRENDAN *turns off the light and leaves.*

Slow fade.

DUBLIN CAROL

Dublin Carol was first performed at the Royal Court Theatre Downstairs, Sloane Square, London on 7 January 2000. The cast was as follows:

MARK   Andrew Scott

JOHN   Brian Cox

MARY   Bronagh Gallagher

Director   Ian Rickson
Designer   Rae Smith
Lighting Designer   Paule Constable
Music   Stephen Warbeck

Characters

JOHN, *late fifties*

MARK, *early twenties*

MARY, *thirties*

The play is set over one day, 24 December:

    Part One: late morning.

    Part Two: early afternoon.

    Part Three: late afternoon.

The action takes place in an office on the Northside of Dublin, around Fairview or the North Strand Road.

Part One

An office. Dublin. The present.

The office is furnished with old wooden desks, carpet,
comfortable chairs, filing cabinets, tasteful paintings, elaborate
lamps. But all a bit old and musty. In one corner is a sink with
cups, teapot, kettle, etc. There is an electric fire. There are
terribly scrawny Christmas decorations. A few fairy lights.
A foot-high plastic Christmas tree on one of the desks. A little
advent calendar with just a few doors left to open.

MARK, a young man of about twenty or twenty-one comes in.
He wears a black suit and an overcoat. He looks a bit wet.
He stands in the office for a few moments by himself, as though
waiting to be told what to do.

Then JOHN comes in. He's in his fifties. He also wears a black
suit and overcoat. He's not quite as wet as MARK.

JOHN. Sorry. I had to make a call. Get your wet gear off,
Mark, yeah?

MARK. Yeah.

JOHN. I'll put the kettle on.

JOHN fills the kettle. MARK takes his coat off and looks for
somewhere to put it. He drapes it over a chair and stands
with his hands in his pockets.

Plug in that old fire there.

MARK goes down beside a desk and plugs the fire in.

You did very well.

MARK. Really?

JOHN. Oh yeah.

JOHN takes off his coat and takes a hanger from a hook
on the door. He hangs his coat up. He takes a towel from
beside the sink and tosses it to MARK. MARK rubs his hair.

Give your head a rub.

MARK. Thanks Mr Plunkett.

JOHN. Sit down there.

MARK sits on a chair. JOHN stays near the sink and farts around with the tea. He takes a small bottle of whiskey from a drawer and pours some into a cup.

I'm not gonna offer you any of this, son. Your ma'd kill me. I'm old. I'll die if I don't drink this.

MARK (*laughs*). That's alright.

JOHN. I have to have a sup of this.

Pause.

You can have a cup of tea in a minute. (*Short pause.*) When the kettle boils up. You know what I mean?

They laugh. (NB: any laughter denoted between the characters need not be literal. Tiny breaths or smiles may suffice and it's up to the actors to find their own rhythm and pitch in rehearsal.)

Yeah . . . There's an old pub there across the road, you know? The Strand.

MARK. Yeah I was in there.

JOHN. Yeah?

MARK. Yeah I was in there last night. After work. My girlfriend came down and met me there.

JOHN. Yeah?

MARK. Yeah. She knew it.

JOHN. Yeah?

MARK. Yeah. She knew it from before. She used to work down there in the stationery place.

JOHN. Oh right. Where's she from?

MARK. Marino.

JOHN. Ah well, then, you know?

MARK. Yeah.

JOHN. Up the road.

MARK. Yeah.

JOHN. She's only down the road. A lot of people would know it. Your man does give the regulars a Christmas drink and all this.

MARK. Yeah. It was fairly busy. A lot of people going home from work.

JOHN. Ah yeah, they do a, they used to always do a nice lunch, and you'd get all the people going in there for their nosh. You used to see a lot of priests going in. And that's, did you ever hear that, that's a sign the food is good, you know?

They laugh.

Because they know what side their bread is buttered on. That's a little hint for you there now. The old girlfriend, ha? Does she still work up there?

MARK. No she's an air hostess.

JOHN. Oh ho!

MARK laughs.

Very 'How's it fuckin' goin' . . . '

MARK (*slightly embarrassed*). Yep.

JOHN. The uniform.

MARK. Yep.

JOHN. Did you meet her on a plane?

MARK. Nah. Met her at a party.

JOHN. With the uniform and all.

MARK (*laughs, thinks*). I don't like the uniform.

JOHN. Why?

MARK. I don't know. It makes her legs look fat.

JOHN. Ah now here. Where are you going with that kind of talk? Bloody air hostess, man.

MARK. Well you're going a bit mad about it.

They laugh.

JOHN. I know. What's her name?

MARK. Kim.

JOHN. Kim?

MARK. Yeah.

JOHN. That's eh, that's not an Irish name.

MARK. Mm. I don't know what it is.

JOHN. Is it short for something?

MARK. I don't know.

JOHN. Kipling or . . . Nn. What's she like?

MARK. Em. She's sort of dark. Like her skin is kind of dark.

JOHN. What, sort of tanned or kind of yellowy?

MARK (*laughs*). Yeah kind of.

JOHN. Was she on her holidays?

MARK. No. She just is.

JOHN. Janey Mack. There's people'd love that, you know?

MARK. Yeah.

JOHN. Are you going out long?

MARK. Going out a year and three months.

JOHN. Oh my God. This is the big one, ha?

MARK. You never know.

JOHN. If it's there, it's there, you know? But ah . . . (*Thinks better of what he is going to say.*) . . . you know? How old are you, son?

MARK. Twenty.

JOHN. Jesus. Twenty. God. I don't know. Grasp the nettle.
(*Short pause.*) But you obviously don't have any trouble
there. In that department.

MARK (*good-naturedly*). Give me a break, will you?

JOHN. I'm sorry. Hangover. Has me chatty. You did very well
today, do you know that?

MARK. Did I really?

JOHN. Oh yeah. Very good. You're a natural.

MARK *grimaces slightly as if to say 'This better not be my
calling.'*

MARK. Do you not find it kind of horrible, though?

JOHN. Ah that person was young, Mark. I'm telling you, it's
not usually like that. People get older, they're naturally kind
of ready for it, you know? And everybody knows that. And
it's all a few quid for the priest and soup and sandwiches in
the Addison Lodge. You know? It's different with old
people. You get used to it. You were very good. Helping that
girl.

MARK (*hoping* JOHN *agrees*). She couldn't drive.

JOHN (*matter-of-factly*). No. (*Sly pause.*) What do you
reckon? Was she a bit on the side.

MARK (*catching on*). Maybe an old girlfriend or something,
alright.

JOHN. He was a drug addict, you know?

MARK. Oh really, yeah?

JOHN. See the amount of fucking young ones? I'd say he was
a right little cunt, d'you ever get that feeling? Three and
four-timing them left right and centre. Did you not see his
little missus. Shooting daggers all round the grave?

MARK. Really?

JOHN. It was a mess! (*Short pause.*) Do you think I'm very
callous, Mark, yeah?

MARK. No.

JOHN. I often think I must be. But with Noel out sick, and me having to run things a little bit. I've been having a . . . *(Although almost certain of something.)* Are you supposed to just fucking . . .

MARK. Yeah . . . ?

JOHN. No I'm just *(As though this is what he's been wondering about.)* you'd think this kettle would never boil. I don't drink loads of tea. It's a thing with it that people go mad to put the kettle on. I know I'm after putting it on now, but we're wet and so on. But people do be falling all over themselves to be giving you tea all the time.

Distant church bells ring out.

Do you go to mass?

MARK. No.

JOHN. The same as meself. Why d'you not go?

MARK. I don't know. It's hard to eh . . . *(Almost unexpectedly deflates.)* Psss. I don't know. I just don't go I suppose.

JOHN. Yeah . . . I haven't gone in years either, you know? Although I feel like I do because there's always mass going on at the funeral. Outside the porch, or sitting in the car like we were today. Go in at the end. Help the poor lads who want to carry the coffin and all this. Nobody carried it today. But you'll get it where they want to. But it should feel like it's a big part of my life because you do always be in churches all the time.

MARK. Well it is, isn't it? Big part of your life. You're more . . . than most people, you know?

JOHN *(slightly vainly, as though they should get the details of his life correct)*. I'm *around* it. You know?

MARK. Yeah . . .

JOHN. Are you a Christmas man?

MARK. Yeah, I suppose I am. I like Christmas.

JOHN. Get the little lady a present and so on.

MARK. Well I suppose you have to, don't you? You know?

JOHN. Ah you have to. Get her a nice jumper or something.

They laugh.

MARK. Get her a nice anorak.

JOHN. Oh she'll be delighted. Nice pair of socks in the pockets. Little surprise, you know?

They laugh.

MARK. God. Imagine.

JOHN. Oh there's lads and they do things like that. Buying the wives cutlery and toasters and all sorts of shite. But then again, a lot of it is shite. You know?

They laugh.

Fucking hairdryers.

They laugh.

You know in the pictures you never see a baldy Indian. In the cowboys and Indians.

MARK (*thinks*). Yeah.

JOHN. That's you don't wash your hair. You never see a bald knacker. You see the itinerants. They let the natural oils do the business. There's not all hairdryers in the caravans and all this.

MARK. Do you have to get many presents?

JOHN. Ah sure not any more. A boy over in England there, and, you know . . . Jesus I never made you any fucking tea.

JOHN *goes to make tea.*

We can't be having that.

MARK. No, it's fine. I have to go.

JOHN. We never did the advent calendar. You do it.

MARK *goes to the advent calendar and opens a little door on it.* JOHN *makes tea for* MARK.

What is it?

MARK. Ahm. It's little angels, like in a choir.

JOHN. A feast of heavenly angels, is it? No it's a host of heavenly angels. 'A feast.' I'm losing the marbles entirely at this stage. Have you gone in to see your Uncle Noel?

MARK. Not yet, no, I haven't. I should go really.

JOHN. Yeah. Ah he's not very well, you know?

MARK. Yeah?

JOHN. Yeah. (*Actively reassuring.*) He'll get better. But just it's not great, in the hospital for Christmas, you know?

MARK. Mmm.

JOHN. But the nurses are great and all that. They help you, you know?

MARK. Yeah.

JOHN. Poor fella. I went in last night. And it was after visiting hours, because of the removal. There was no one kind of in there. Not even the full lights on and all this. And I think whatever they do to try and have people home at Christmas, there was only one other fella there in the ward. Some auldfella. And he was asleep. And Noelly was there with the telly on, only low, watching some terrible shite altogether. And I was sitting there with him, and he was very tired from all the tests and all this they were doing on him. And it just felt like I should be trying to get him out. Like a jailbreak or something.

They smile.

It was all kind of blue, and just the light coming off the telly, (*Ominously.*) on the shiny floor. Aw, it's a different world. You're very helpless. Like the doctors say it's all looking good. But ah . . . Do you know what it was? It was kind of embarrassing. Having to ask if you can do your toilet and all. He had a bit of an upset stomach. From whatever tablets they give him. And instead of asking the nurse for a bit of something, he was lying there and kind of bearing up, you know?

They laugh.

And I said, ah, here, I'll lash out to the nurse. Nurse sitting out there on her own at the station. And I go 'Your man in here is feeling a bit yucky, you know?' And she was grand, like. No problem. She gave him this bit of medicine, there, the sad eyes looking up at her. (*Laughs.*) It's terrible, isn't it. Grown up man. Although. Maybe we all like a bit of pampering. What do you think?

MARK (*laughs*). We might. Yeah.

JOHN. Mm. He was great for me. I was very very messy at one time, you know? And he gave me a start here. Got me back into a normal . . . He's a good man. But he will, he'll get out, and he'll be back here. Might give you a bit of a better start here if you want. More permanent. He'll need people.

MARK. Yeah. Well I think I'm gonna try to go to college next year.

JOHN. Oh very good!

MARK. Yeah.

JOHN. Yeah. (*Beat.*) Your mam was saying you were kind of kicking around a bit. No offence.

MARK. No, she's right, you're right. I have been, you know? Been out of school for three years now. And whatever I've been doing. I haven't eh you know.

JOHN. You see, you haven't settled in anywhere.

MARK. Yeah.

JOHN. Well, Jesus, don't worry about it yet, you're only twenty years of age. It's not like you've killed somebody!

They laugh.

You'll find your niche. This was mine.

MARK. Is it not any more?

JOHN. Aw no, it is, it has been, I mean. When I found it. And if college isn't starting until next September or whenever it is, you could do a lot worse than this.

MARK. Mm.

JOHN. It can be sad. But there is a dignity to it. (*Short pause.*) Because you're trying to find the dignity. You're trying to afford people a bit of respect in their last little bit with their family and the people around them. Funeral is for the people left behind. That's what it's for. It's not for the dead person. I don't think. Mm. When I go though – very small.

MARK. Yeah?

JOHN. Keeping it all very quiet.

MARK (*with good-humoured amusement*). Yeah?

JOHN. Spare people the old hassle.

MARK. But what if people want to pay their respect to you?

JOHN. Ah respect is no use to you when you're gone. If you don't earn it while you're alive, don't be looking for it just because you've happened to die. I never really did any great things. In fact, I've done many things which, to tell you the truth, I'm very very ashamed of. And if you've let people down, don't be wanting them to be all crowding around talking about what a brilliant fella you were, at your funeral, you know? (*With a certain resigned emphatic quality.*) I've seen enough funerals where people have been genuinely heartbroken for me to expect for people to be, you know, mourning me and all this. I just want to slip away, you know? Very quiet. Under cover of darkness.

They give a little laugh.

The great escape.

MARK. Yeah. Very morbid.

They laugh.

JOHN. Well. It fucking is. You know?

They laugh.

Good Jaysus, these decorations are scaldy.

MARK (*laughs*). They're not the best, alright.

JOHN. I don't know. What do we want? Flashing . . . fairy lights . . . But of course you know, we have to be a bit cool because we have so many people in here recently bereaved. We can't have flashing lights and 'Ding Dong Merrily on High' and (*With physicality.*) 'Ah! How's it going?' You know?

MARK *spits out his tea laughing.*

Ah now here. Tea going everywhere and everything now. God, you get those fellas crooning all bloody Christmas. It's a real slippers-and-pipe job. In the rocking chair. Do you ever see that?

MARK (*a little laugh*). Yeah.

JOHN. Jays, it was great. I used to love all that, you know? The bloody lengths I used to go to. I was worse than the kids. Hiding presents all over the place. Leaving out cake and a drink for Santy. I spent an hour one Christmas Eve telling them Santy didn't like sherry. He liked Macardle's.

They laugh.

Because it was for me, you know? (*Pause.*) Tch. Jaysus. You know?

Pause.

Long time ago now, you know?

Silence. MARK *seems to get ready to go.*

MARK. I better eh . . .

JOHN (*as though stopping him*). D'you want a biscuit, here, did you have your breakfast?

MARK. I'm grand, I don't really ever eat breakfast.

JOHN. What?

MARK. I have to go anyway. I have to do some stuff.

JOHN (*almost desperately opening a packet of biscuits, offering them to* MARK). Well, you know, you have to . . . you can't be . . . Like I don't care what you do normally. But you're standing out in the cold now. You have to have a bit of fuel in you. Keep you going you know, on your feet all day. In all weathers. Noelly got me in the habit. I used to be like you. I'd nearly be puking if someone put a load of food in front of me in the morning. God, I didn't know how people could do it.

MARK *finally has a biscuit and has to stay a little longer.* JOHN's *slight hysteria subsides and he relaxes, becoming direct with* MARK.

At the same time, I was at a time, in my life, where I was very dependent on drink. D'you understand me?

MARK (*affirmative*). Mm hm.

JOHN. Not that I don't drink now. I still drink. You know? But not in the way that I used to. And the way I was then, Jaysus you'd wake up in the morning and you'd still be very pissed. But horrible. I'm telling you this because this is the story of how I met your Uncle Noel, yeah?

MARK. Yeah, yeah.

JOHN. You'd want to die. All you could do, this'd be the routine, was hang on 'til opening time, in you'd go. One or two lads in the same predicament. The big red faces, and the big swollen fuckin' heads. God the first one or two pints'd knock the fuckin' head off you, but then one or two more, and you'd be feeling a bit better, head home or wherever you call home, you'd probably be able to lie down and get a bit of kip then. Up you'd get, six or seven and off out into the night. Winter nights and summer nights. Winter nights the steam coming off everybody's wet coats. And the stink of all those dirty bastards leaning into you and snoring in the bar. Summer nights. God, it's amazing what the weather does, nothing's as bad, is it? You'd actually be making the effort. Having a shave and every fucking thing. Clean shirt. Down on the road, waiting on the bus in the summer breeze. Good God. (*Short pause.*)

Now I wasn't always like that and I haven't been like that since. But this is because of, thanks to Noelly. Bloody fucking . . . you know, got me. Sorted me out. Got talking to him in the pub across the road. You know what he's like. All . . . (*Raises himself up.*) You know, the bearing. You know?

They smile.

MARK. Yeah.

JOHN. He was one of them people. Still is. Always sat there on his own, reading the paper. Very much his own man, and keeping himself to himself. But what you'd notice about him was that he seemed to know everybody. They'd all be saying hello to him, he'd be very much on for a quick chat, crack a joke or whatever. But then back to himself. Very much at peace. And one time I asked someone, you know, who is your man? What does he do? An' when they said, 'Undertaker' you know. It was like. 'Oh right.' That makes sense. I can see that. And one time, whatever happened, I was there and there wasn't very many people there and I was with someone who knew him. This was very civilised drinking. That's why that was always a great pub. The staff were very good. Very discreet. Never any messing. I've been in some terrible fucking places. Filthy dirty places. Big rows all the time and all. Fucking barman would have a mattress down behind the bar, fucking be living there and every fucking thing, you know? I mean, Jesus. But across the road there, used to be called Hannigan's then. Very good. And whatever happened this time, there were very few people there and Noel came in and sat up at the bar like everyone else and he was chatting away, very dry wit. Had us all in stitches. And he bought me a drink and I got chatting to him on his own. He had a great, and he still has it, a great listening quality, you have it as well.

MARK *smiles a little self-consciously.*

And I was chatting away, this and that and I began to tell him a bit about myself. Not in any fucking-stupid-pisshead-very-sorry-for-myself way or anything, anything, like that. But I explained that I was in a bit of a mess. I had gotten myself into a terrible mess. This is many years ago. And

I had gone to the stage where I was down to the very last bit of my savings, and I was out of work because I'd basically, no two ways about it, I'd hit the bottle goodo. And I was in and out of my house and I was going to end up on the, the, fucking skids, you know? Be a tramp, you know?

JOHN *is slightly distressed for a second. Just a glimpse of something, a flash in the face.*

It was an extremely bad situation. (*Short pause.*) Now to be fair, I wasn't looking for anything off him. Sure you wouldn't expect for someone to do what he did. I was just basically telling him the truth. And I was generally getting things off my chest. And right there, he says come on back and have a bite and this. Went back, came in here, sat down like where you are and he offers me a job.

You know. Give me a start. And eh . . . God I didn't want to let him down. But your pride kicks in as well. I didn't want to be a charity case on anybody's back. But he sensed that too, you know? And he was able to phrase it properly, more like he needed me more than I needed him, and it was simply a fortuitous thing that had happened – us meeting up. And there was a spare room and all this.

I was so tired. Not just from it being the night-time and everything. But in general. Up he goes and lights a fire in the room. Gives me a pair of pyjamas. What was I like?

They smile.

I was like something out of Peter Pan and Wendy or something. All I needed now was a little Teddy bear.

They laugh.

Jesus. But fair dues. What got me on to this?

Oh yes! Breakfast!

They laugh.

He gets me up in the morning. God. A huge big fry. Rashers and eggs and everything. Pots of tea. Loads of toast. And it got me in the habit. Which is the point I was making.

Mmm.

MARK. What was the job?

JOHN. Same as you today. Carrying wreaths. Lifting out the
coffin. And excuse the pun, but generally looking grave.
Looking grave and sombre. I'm not a mortician, now, like
Noel. There were two other men that were here then. Old
Paddy McDermott and Andy Stafford. They're gone now,
retired and everything . . . Quiet fellas, you know? And
you couldn't bring the subject up . . . But, you see, Noelly
would take us all over for a few pints a couple of nights
a week. It was like, fucking, like a supervised drink. These
were older fellas now. Big lads. Low gruff . . . (*Hunches
over.*) . . . voices. And Noelly would buy a few rounds, you
know. And I often wondered if, the two boys were . . . if
they'd got these jobs in the same way, you know, that I did.
Like your Uncle Noel was some . . . He's a very good man,
you know?

MARK. Mmm.

JOHN. The more I think about them now. Years on from them.
I always remember them as very battered men. They were
like they'd had the shit kicked out of them, you know?

MARK *is genuinely interested in all of this. His prospects
lie ahead of him, and what the world has in store.*

I think Andy had even been in prison for something. But
you'd never ask. But they weren't know-alls like you get in
so many pubs in Dublin. God, there's some terrible fucking
eejits. The fellas who fucked your ma and forgave your da
for letting them. You know?

MARK *nearly loses his tea again.*

Did you never hear that one? Jesus there's some awful men.
I'm a Dublin man. Sometimes I wish maybe if I'd lived out
in the country, what the hell would I've been like. Probably
the same. Bullshit artist.

They smile.

But eh . . . he'd take us over for a pint. But we did see some
awful stuff at the same time. Suicides and a woman been
killed one time, you know?

MARK. What's the worst thing you've seen?

JOHN. Baby born down a toilet.

MARK. What?!

JOHN. Ah this fucking thing, young girl got pregnant from
some fella, some uncle or someone. Course she had no idea
what was going on. One because she was fourteen and two
because a lot of these people are very stupid and nobody
thought there was anything wrong with her. Middle of
the night then, she wakes up. In labour. On to the jacks
for a few hours. She tried to flush it away but it blocked
up the plumbing. I didn't see it down the toilet. I only saw
it after.

But ahm . . . And this is the other side of it. I was once over
picking up a job in Terenure. This house, wasn't much to
look at outside. But inside it was all beautiful. Set back
from the road. All the walls knocked in on the inside.

MARK. Open plan.

JOHN. Yes. And big bright airy windows. Very peaceful with
the wind going through the leaves out there in the back.
And a big long wooden table when we arrived. And a bottle
of the hard stuff and a couple of glasses there for us – this
was a suicide and the guards had been and it looked all
fairly cut and dry. Little old man up in the bed. Tiny wasted
away. Sleeping pills and booze there beside the bed. Note
and all this. He was, or had been, sick from cancer. And
took his own life. Very calm there. Very peaceful. Me and
Andy sort of looked down at him in the bed, but we didn't
move him for a while. We just sort of went and sat at the
big table and stole a nip of the scotch or whatever it was
was there. Very relaxed or something. All around were
plants and statues of what do you call it? Buddha. (*Pause.*)
Mmm. Paddy. Andy. Broken noses and generally battered
by life. But never the complaint. Never the fucking moaning
Minnie. Unlike my good self. Eejit boy. That's the super-
hero I'd be. 'We need to have this fucked up immediately!
Quick! Get Eejit Boy!' Who'd you be?

MARK. Horny Man.

They burst out laughing.

JOHN The man with the horn, ha?

MARK. Yeah.

They are quiet for a moment.

JOHN. You might as well be on your way. Come and get your money later.

MARK. Alright.

JOHN. Come in in the afternoon.

MARK. Okay.

JOHN. Good man and well done.

MARK *leaves.*

JOHN *puts the cups on the sink. He goes and puts his own coat on, an anorak. He takes the bottle of whiskey and puts the top on it. He stretches. He unplugs the fire. He coughs.*

(*Absent-mindedly as he leaves.*) 'Buddha.'

The lights fade.

End of Part One.

Part Two

MARY *comes into the office. She is in her thirties and seems very tired. She looks around a little bit. She then sits.*

JOHN *comes into the office. He carries a bag from the off-licence.*

JOHN. I'm sorry. I had to run across the road.

He takes a bottle of whiskey from the bag and opens it. He is dying to get a drink into him.

MARY. You still . . .

JOHN. Oh nowhere near! This is shocking news Mary. And I had to get a few bits for the Christmas. Will you have a drink?

MARY. It's a bit early.

JOHN. Ah Jaysus, shocking news though. For me.

MARY. Just give me a little bit.

JOHN. Yes. I'm glad. Not drinking on my own.

JOHN gives them both a drink of neat whiskey in old mugs. JOHN shoots his back in one, his eyes nearly coming out on stalks. He immediately pours himself another. MARY takes a sip from hers. It's too strong for her.

MARY. Can I have a drop of water?

JOHN. Oh yes, of course.

He takes her drink over to the sink and pours some water in.

We're really closed but I have to give a youngfella his wages later. So handier here.

MARY. That's fine.

JOHN. This is terrible news. I'll have to sort out going in.

MARY. Oh you *have* to . . . ?

JOHN. Well I should I think. I think I should.

MARY. Of course you should! What are you talking about?

JOHN. I'm just saying I have to go in.

MARY. Of course you have to.

JOHN. What's wrong?

MARY. Just you make it like such a chore. For you.

JOHN. No. Just I've been in and out seeing Noel, the man who runs this business. And it's just. Going to the hospital. I don't know. I didn't mean anything.

MARY (*softens a little*). Come with me today.

JOHN. What time are you going in at?

MARY. I could pick you up at five or something. (*Pause.*) Okay?

JOHN (*awkward, guarded*). Is Paul gonna come home?

MARY. He's coming on Monday.

JOHN. How is he, alright, yeah?

MARY. The same as me, just can't believe it.

JOHN. But in general.

MARY. He fixes motorbikes, with this friend of his.

JOHN. English fella.

MARY. Yeah.

JOHN. What, like you go over?

MARY. I just been twice. I was there in the summer.

JOHN. But he's alright.

MARY. Yeah he's . . . He's the same as he was. Drifts along. He's getting like you though, more and more.

JOHN. Yeah? God.

A slightly awkward moment passes between them which
MARY *breaks, just for something to say.*

MARY. I don't know if I could live there.

JOHN. Yeah?

MARY (*direct, almost without expression*). It's like Coronation
Street. That's what it's like. That's what it looks like.

JOHN. Yeah?

MARY. The little streets. All little terraced houses and all. Up
and down these hills. When I was there. Every day it was
you go around the corner and either get a pizza or an Indian
or a Chinese.

JOHN. Out of the take-away.

MARY (*regaining expression and lucidity*). Yeah. Yeah. Just do
that all the time. His friend Craig comes around and they
stand in this little back garden drinking beer and tinkering
around with motorbikes. I used to go and sit in this
graveyard.

JOHN. How is he getting like me?

MARY. The way he says things and nods. The way he stands
in the pub and things like that.

JOHN. And what do yous say? About me and all that?

MARY. He doesn't . . . He doesn't say anything. About you.

JOHN *exhales deeply.*

You look much older.

JOHN. Yeah?

MARY *nods.*

I am older, you know? D'you want another drink?

MARY. No.

JOHN *pours himself one.*

JOHN. Little smartener.

MARY. Yeah. (*Again softens a little, brings* JOHN *in . . .*) He has this horrible girlfriend.

JOHN. Yeah?

MARY. Yeah well she's not really any more. But she doesn't leave him alone. She's a little scrawny thing. Her hair is in bits. And she has terrible acne because she only eats pub grub and chocolate. She's like a little monkey. She gets pissed and comes round to his house. It was very funny. She came around one day and we had to lie down in the living room near the wall so she couldn't see us. Me and Paul and Craig. God, it was hard not make any noise, I was bursting out laughing. I thought I was going to wet myself. She was there for ages. One of the neighbours even came out and asked her what was wrong with her. God it was awful. She's a bit mad, like, I think.

JOHN. Tch.

They look at each other.

MARY. She caught us in one night. It was so hot we had the front door open. Because there's no hall, just the front room where we were sitting. In she walks. It was awful. She plonked herself down and started just talking. It was so weird. She wouldn't go. I just went up to bed. But she was there in the morning. She only went when me and Paul pretended to go out.

JOHN (*a little laugh*). Mmmm.

Pause.

MARY. Mmm.

JOHN. How are you doing? I'm sorry, this is very hard.

MARY. Yeah, I'm . . . I'm working in Dunnes. In Stephen's Green.

JOHN. Oh right. Okay.

MARY. It's alright, you know. It's okay.

JOHN. Well that's alright, isn't it?

MARY (*looks around, no pause*). I'll have to do all this . . . funeral . . .

Silence.

JOHN. What else are you doing?

MARY. I don't know. Sometimes I drive down the country. Wonder what the fuck I'm doing there and come back.

JOHN. You remember down in Limerick. Where we used to go.

MARY. Yeah. When Paul lost his shoes.

JOHN. Oh God yeah. Jesus. The ructions.

MARY. Mmm.

JOHN. We had some great times down there. You might have been too young.

MARY. No I remember. I remember Paul losing his shoes. I remember standing in the middle of a load of nettles one time. Couldn't go anywhere without being stung. Just standing there in this little sleeveless dress I loved. Getting stung to bits. You came in through the nettles and lifted me out.

JOHN. Yeah.

MARY. I remember one night. We were all in the house and you hadn't come home. Auntie Rita wanted Mam to ring the guards. Or ring the hospitals to see what had happened. But Mam knew you'd come back.

JOHN. I was gone to the pictures.

MARY. What?!

JOHN. I mean first.

MARY. Yeah, not all night.

JOHN. Yeah I went to the pub.

MARY. Oh Duh . . .

JOHN. Yeah well that's where I was.

MARY. Course you were.

JOHN. I used to get caught down the country. Up home they kick you out at eleven. But you'd be chancing a quick one like that, those boys'll (*i.e., barmen in the country*) serve you 'til two o'clock in the morning. So you'd think you were catching them for a quick one after the pictures. But the door'd be locked and it was just getting going.

MARY. Do you know how many years it is, since I've seen you?

JOHN. I don't know.

MARY. That day I met you on Henry Street and we went for a cup of coffee.

JOHN. Oh yeah . . . ?

MARY. That's ten years ago.

JOHN. Okay.

MARY. And you're still, you're still making bloody excuses about a night in Limerick, what twenty-five years ago. I just, I don't believe it.

JOHN. Well, I'm telling you.

MARY. I know. But. Here I am. I don't know what to call you. Our lives are . . .

JOHN. It happens a lot.

MARY (*marvelling at him*). But you're still, here making excuses.

JOHN. But what do you want me to say?

MARY. I don't know. But it's like you're treating me like a fool. 'I'd get caught . . . A quick one after the pictures . . . ' If you even went to the pictures. When Mam was in hospital having Paul I remember Auntie Rita came to stay. You slept in with me. And you had a bottle of something up in the wardrobe. I woke up and you were sitting down against the radiator.

JOHN. I couldn't sleep.

MARY. See again, there's an excuse.

JOHN. Of course there's an excuse. You think I'd deliberately want to hurt you? I wish it was different. But that's what I needed to do.

MARY. Yeah but do you not . . . (*The rest is unspeakable.*)

Silence. JOHN *explodes.*

JOHN. What do you want me to say about it? I'm not going to just say, 'I'm sorry' – because of the fucking enormity of all the fucking things I did. It's not enough. Jesus. I know. I know. I think about everybody. You're telling me Helen is going to die?! Where am I supposed to be? I remember her years ago. Jesus, how can I go and look at that? Should I, even?

MARY. You're her husband.

JOHN. I'm not her fucking husband! What kind of fucking husband am I? That's all gone.

MARY. It'd mean a lot to her.

Pause.

JOHN. She wants me to go?

MARY *nods.* JOHN *closes his eyes and hangs his head.*

Tch.

He makes a long hissing sigh.

What goes through people's minds? (*Short pause.*) Is she in a state, like?

MARY. No she's exhausted just. You'd want to see her if it was you.

JOHN. No I wouldn't. I'd want it all over quick as possible.

MARY. No I don't believe that.

JOHN (*tone of 'That's your opinion'*). Well.

MARY. I'd want to see you.

Pause.

JOHN. Why?

Pause.

MARY. Because I love you.

Long pause.

JOHN. Why do you love me?

MARY. I can't help it. I always think about you. And I . . .
(*Matter-of-factly.*) I hate you too.

JOHN. I think about you as well, you know? Don't do this.

Pause.

MARY. I had this boyfriend. He wasn't my boyfriend. I don't
know what I was thinking. He was, this friend of mine at
work, he was her brother. He was a big . . . they're from
Kildare. He was a big culchie, teacher. Primary school
teacher. I met him when we were out one night. There's this
place, Major Tom's. I was. I just wanted something to
happen. He was there. A big shiny red face. I didn't . . .
I wasn't serious about him. I saw him a few times. Drinking
stupid cocktails around those places up there around the
centre. And I just came up the steps with him one night,
into the street. And whatever it was, the way the buildings
looked, it took me back in time. And I felt that, you . . .
I felt that you were with me. And this guy Ger, he was
always pissed. He wanted me to go back to his house with
him. And I know this is weird, but it was like he was,
compared to you, even as a messer, compared to you, he
was such a fucking amateur.

They give a little laugh.

Do you know? That even in the morning all he'd complain
about would be his hangover and how he had copybooks
to correct. Where you'd be looking for money to hit the
bottle . . .

JOHN. Which is terrible . . .

They are smiling a little, JOHN *shaking his head.*

For who I was and who you were and what I should have
been looking for money for.

MARY. Sometimes I smell you. Everything comes back.

JOHN. I know.

MARY. I can smell it now.

JOHN. It's Brut.

Pause.

MARY. Do you still see . . . Carol . . . ?

JOHN. Oh, no. I don't even want to talk about it.

MARY. I know she didn't take you away. I know she looked
after you.

JOHN. She kept me going. She liked me too much. Warts and
all. Horrible characteristics and everything. That was the
problem. Would've watched me kill myself if that was what
I wanted.

MARY. I remember the weekend you left.

JOHN. Don't . . .

MARY. It was a Friday, you came to collect me from school.
And it was usually Mam and I came out and whatever was
going on, it was you instead of her. And I remember you
could hardly stand without swaying. You were hanging on
to the railings and we went to get the bus. And the smell of
drink off you.

JOHN. I know.

MARY. And you didn't know what the hell you were doing,
and we went and got the bus on the wrong side of the road.

JOHN. This is all a long time ago.

MARY. And we went into town! And you couldn't talk
properly or anything.

JOHN. I know.

MARY. Jesus. Neither of us knew where the hell we were. I was only seven. And you must've been drinking for days.

JOHN. I know.

MARY. And you took me into a pub! I don't know how you managed to, but you got a drink. I don't think the barman saw me. You were up on a stool. I was down on the ground and all I could do was take out my school books. I remember looking at my Religion book and wanting Jesus to come and get me. You were like somebody else.

JOHN. I know.

MARY. There was a row or something and you fell on top of me.

JOHN. This is awful.

MARY. A ban guard took me home.

JOHN. I know. Terrible things happen. You have a temper and you're not talking to someone. And you calm down and try to keep your heart, fucking, somehow open. But you go and hit the fucking bottle. And you make everything fucking worse. I know you want me to say I'm sorry.

MARY. No . . .

JOHN (*although calm, he is trawling a black place*). But I can hardly remember anything. I was in a very bad state. I don't want to make any excuses, but Jesus Christ! I was in hell. I was in agony. And nobody knew. And I didn't know what to do about it. You don't know. I am sorry. I am sorry. I'm sorry about the whole stinking business. I think about it now and I want to puke. I wish I'd never been born. It's all been awful.

MARY. No. It hasn't all been awful.

JOHN. No. It's been awful for me and I made it terrible for you and your mother and Paul. God. There was one morning I was with Carol, down there in her house, down there in Sybil Hill. And whatever was wrong with me, I was after getting out of bed. I was in bed with this woman,

Mary! You were in school. And I went over to the window.
She had these venetian blinds with tassles on the end of
them. And it was these tassles. I was looking out at her bit
of a garden there and these tassles. Tassles on the blinds.
And whatever it was, I knew I'd fucking blown it, you
know? Because although I'd never would've given a flying
shite about blinds and tassles on them it was just something
your mother would never have bought. Because it was
crummy. It was gaudy or whatever. And I suddenly felt like
I was miles and miles away from you and Helen and Pauly.
And I knew I couldn't go back. Because I was dirty. I was a
dirty filthy dirty man. And you're making me think about it.
I'm often wondering where Pauly is. Over in England and
all. And if he's thinking about me. God I feel like my brain
is going to burst. And you come in and you're so like your
mother, and I often, just sometimes wish you'd just fuck off.

MARY. I know.

JOHN. There was this day. I woke up in Carol's house, sick
and everything all over my clothes. And I took some of her
husband's clothes. She kept them! Oh it was awful. She
kept them for all those years. He'd been dead longer than
they'd been married. It was like a nightmare. And I put on
his gear and started walking home. Hoping to God, for once
that your mother would be there! I was changing
everything. I needed her to be there. I was going to change
it all and get help and basically apologise to everybody. And
there I was coming down the road, and I saw her face at the
window, looking out, and I was going 'Yes!' 'It's all over,
I'll never go this low again . . . ' And I got in the door and
went to where she was there, but it wasn't her, it was the
breadboard or something there against the window. So. Do
you know what I did?

MARY. I can guess.

JOHN. Yeah, off out on another bender. In a dead man's
clothes? 'I'll never go this low?' I'd managed to go even
further.

Short pause.

I knew when it was happening. At the beginning. There was a lot of money knocking about in those days. And a lot of parties. And if I had second sight or something. I knew I was absolutely fucked. Be there in someone's new house at Christmas. People all enjoying themselves, all the fucking wives expecting babies. And it was like I could see the soul of the party or something. The kick off the first few drinks. Like the soul of the party was like a beautiful girl dancing through the room. And then, of course by the end of the night when I'd basically insulted and alienated everyone, the soul of the party was this old fucking cripple that didn't even have the energy to complain or ask for help any more. Me leaving those places, the fucking silence behind me as I left was . . . fucking . . . deafening.

MARY. I'm not . . . I didn't come here to hurt you.

JOHN. What do you mean?

MARY. I don't know. I feel like I'm hurting you.

JOHN. You can't hurt me. What have I done? (*Short pause. He's trying to express that she seems very real to him all of a sudden.*) You know? I'm looking at you. I'm looking at you there, you know?

MARY. Do you want me to go? I don't want to go.

JOHN (*he's belting back the whiskey*). Oh fucking hell.

MARY. Do you . . . ever wish you could . . . go back and have it all different?

JOHN. Go back? No way. I just wish it never happened I don't want anything to exist, you know? Of what happened.

MARY. You don't want me to exist?

JOHN. Not like this! Not with me as your . . . dad.

MARY (*matter-of-factly, no malice*). I'm not happy. (*Either.*)

JOHN. I know. Don't! This is horrible.

MARY. But I don't know if it's your fault. I'm kind of an eejit, as well on my own, like, you know?

Pause. They laugh.

You know?

JOHN. You're an eejit in your own right . . .

MARY (*a little laugh*). Yeah.

JOHN. Oh God . . . Well I know where you got it.

MARY. What was Mum like?

JOHN *pours them more drink.*

JOHN. I don't know. I don't know. Quiet. Embarrassed. This is mad. I always felt sorry for her.

MARY. Is that why you were with her?

JOHN. Maybe. I was always sort of fucking perverse. You know? Doing things for the sheer hell of it. Doing stupid things just to sort of see what'd happen.

MARY. Were you just pretending. To love her?

JOHN. I don't know. No. Love . . . What the fuck is that, you know. Ah you just generally get into a sort of a routine. Just . . . Are you . . . se close?

MARY. Yeah.

MARY *starts crying.*

Sorry.

She gets a tissue from her bag, wiping her nose.

I'm just thinking about her.

Pause.

You know, whatever kind of happened to her, because of you and all that. It, whatever way, she had a great strength or something, because of it.

JOHN. Okay.

MARY. There was humour, even, you know?

JOHN. Yeah.

MARY. I'm talking about her in the past already.

JOHN. Well that's . . . you know, you want to get it over with.

MARY. I know I love her, you know?

JOHN. You're full of fucking loving everybody today and all that. Yeah?

MARY (*gently*). You're horrible. Were you always this horrible?

JOHN. I don't mean it.

MARY. She was very lenient and all, you know? On Paul. God, he was a handful. The guards were looking for him and everything, you know?

JOHN. For what?

MARY. Ah he told some ban guard to go fuck herself. In town somewhere.

JOHN. What happened?

MARY. Ah I don't know. She told him to be quiet coming out of a pub or something.

JOHN. Is he a fucking eeejit, is he?

MARY. No! He's great. But I remember Mum sitting at the kitchen table laughing and lighting up a fag. And I remember thinking about her. Right then. And knowing that I loved her. Right in that moment. That's how I know. And I was thinking about you. And I was thinking that you'd be really good friends. And it was sort of a pity or something that you were a man and a woman, you know. Like if you could have both been men, or both been women. I don't know. I just remember that, you know?

JOHN. Or if we were just bloody older. You know? Or maybe being older doesn't even make any difference. You just have to be good, don't you? That's the thing. The man who owns this business was very good to me. I've never been good to anybody. There's something I can't help it. I needed like a teacher or something. The man who runs this business, Noel, he's in hospital having tests done, right? And he's such a kind and a, a, a good person. He doesn't deserve to be sick, nobody does, you know? But there I was, visiting him there. And do you know what was going through my mind? I was going, part of me was, it was like a little tune, I didn't know what it was until I listened to it. I was thinking, 'Here you are all tucked up in hospital, all fucking not well and all this. And I'm up and about, bullshitting for Ireland, rapping along with barmen, and you never hurt a fly. But you're a stupid cunt, because you're sick. You're a wanker, because you're all weak and sick there, taking your medicine.' I felt like I hated him because the poor bastard isn't well. You see, that's mean. That's what I have.

MARY. I don't think that matters. I . . . I don't care.

JOHN. Well I blow my own fucking mind.

MARY. You were sick too. You were sick in your head.

JOHN. I was just sick of my fucking self.

MARY. But that's . . . that's the same.

JOHN (*slightly dismissive*). Yeah, yeah.

MARY (*as though wanting to prove she is like him*). Everybody hated me.

JOHN. What do you mean?

MARY. I was a weird girl.

JOHN. No you weren't.

MARY. When I got older. You'd see me walking around the estate on my own, walking the dog and having a smoke.

JOHN. What dog?

MARY. We got a dog. Snoopy.

JOHN. Really? It's like I feel like I have a dog now.

MARY. He's dead.

JOHN. Okay.

MARY. People used to say that girl's not right.

JOHN. People are only stupid. Ganging up on you.

MARY. I didn't care. I liked it. It made me feel like I was closer to you because I was sort of like you.

JOHN (*shakes his head slowly*). Em.

MARY (*reading him*). But I was only playing at it.

JOHN. You didn't destroy your life. But someone saved me. You know?

MARY. I think that's what I was looking for.

JOHN. You don't need it.

Pause.

MARY. What *happened* to you?

Pause.

JOHN. Boredom. Loneliness. A feeling of basically being out of step with everybody else. Fear. Anxiety. Tension. And of course, a disposition to generally liking the whole fucking thing of drinking until you pass out.

MARY. But what were you worried about?

Pause.

JOHN. I just always felt like people were judging me. I just always felt guilty.

MARY. Why?

JOHN. I don't know. Why do all these young ... drug addicts ... I see people my generation. You see them there in their suit jackets. Sitting on some street corner. Begging for money for drink. You think they don't know it's a short term solution? They know. But the long term is terrifying. Failure reaching up and grabbing you. We were brought up like that a little bit. You know? That we were all going to hell or somewhere. You know?

Short pause.

My dad used to beat the living daylights out of my mother, you know? (*Pause.*) He used to come in and hammer the fucking head off her. Tusssss. And you're only a young boy. You're fucking hiding under the bed, you'd hear him come in roaring. And . . . It wasn't that I was going, 'I'm too young to do anything.' It was something else. I was just . . . shit scared. And I let her take it. So he wouldn't hit me. That feeling went away, when I got older. He became a little frail old man and stopped all that shenanigans. And I fucking just generally forgot about it, you know? But then, years later, when you were born, right? I started to feel again like I was a . . . coward. Do you see I thought the world was a bad place and that someone was going to come and attack us.

MARY. Who?

JOHN. I don't know. But somewhere in me. I knew . . . I'd let you . . . and your mammy . . . down. That if we were attacked. I knew deep down in me, that I'd run away and leave yous to it. You a little baby. And your mother like a little squirrel or something.

MARY. No one was going to attack us.

JOHN. I knew that! But this was a thing that I couldn't help feeling. And it was a terrible fucking feeling to have. And I just believed in it. And I sort of, let yous all down, just *to get it over with*. Or something.

Pause.

I don't understand it.

Pause.

MARY. You could do her funeral.

JOHN. Oh No! No! Mary, no!

MARY. Is that . . .

JOHN. Aw God, Jesus, no . . .

MARY. That's . . . yeah?

JOHN. I couldn't.

MARY. I know.

JOHN. Bad enough, seeing her, but putting her down, in the muck, for fuck's sake Mary.

MARY. Okay.

JOHN. Yeah. There in her dressing gown?! A man in his pyjamas is bad enough. But a woman there in her nightdress. Very much a lady and not a man. And the betrayal and the guilt and everything written all over our fucking faces.

MARY. Don't drink any more.

JOHN. What?

MARY. Don't drink any more before you see her. Be sober, alright?

JOHN. I am sober.

MARY. Yeah but don't drink any more. (*She becomes upset.*) Please.

JOHN (*aggravated*). Okay. Alright. Jesus.

MARY. I'm sorry.

JOHN. No. Oh God!

MARY. Don't see her if . . . you can't.

JOHN (*inhales deeply*). Oh Mary.

MARY. I'll say I couldn't see you or . . .

    JOHN *puts his hand to his face.*

    Okay? (*Short pause.*) I'll tell her I couldn't find you.

JOHN (*exhales*). No.

MARY. I'll help you. We'll go together.

    She wants to go near him. But stays where she is.

    Dad.

    JOHN *looks at her.*

    I'll help you. I'll be with you.

JOHN (*accepting*). Yeah. (*Beat.*) Yeah.

    There's a long pause. In which neither know what to say.

MARY. I'll call here at five.

JOHN. Okay.

MARY (*as much to convince herself as him*). It'll be alright.
It'll be alright.

JOHN. I . . . want to make it up to you.

MARY. Nnn . . . (*Unable to take any more.*) I'm gonna call
back at five. Okay, Dad?

JOHN. I'll be here.

She stays for a moment. And then leaves. JOHN *stands
there.*

The lights fade. End of Part Two.

Part Three

We hear the bells chiming. Four o'clock. JOHN *is slumped in a chair. Three-quarters of the whiskey is gone. He sleeps in a drunken stupor. There is a soft knocking at the door.*

MARK (*off*). Mr Plunkett?

> MARK *opens the door and steps in. He is in casual gear now, and consequently looks younger.*

> Mr Plunkett?

> JOHN *is startled.*

JOHN. What? Paul?

MARK. It's Mark.

JOHN. What are you doing? I haven't gone to the bank.

MARK. Oh. Okay.

JOHN. What time is it?

MARK. Are you alright?

JOHN. Have I missed the bank? What time is it?

MARK. It's five past four.

JOHN. Bollocks. Ah for fuck's sake. I'm sorry.

> JOHN *fishes into his pockets.*

> Are you waiting on it? How much are you owed?

MARK. Forget about it.

JOHN. Ah for fuck's sake, I'm sorry. Here. What's this?

> JOHN *counts some money out of his pocket. It's all different notes bundled in little balls.*

I'm just, I'm sorry, I've had a horrible . . . What's this?
Look there's thirty . . . five . . . Ah I'm sorry.

MARK. Ah it's okay.

JOHN. Will that do you?

MARK. Ah yeah, no, that's grand.

JOHN. I have to go.

JOHN *tries to get his coat. He knocks some furniture over,*
MARK *helps him.*

MARK. Are you okay?

JOHN. I need the toilet.

MARK *gets him to the toilet.*

Will you put the kettle on?

MARK. Yeah. Sure.

JOHN *goes into the toilet.* MARK *puts water in the kettle*
and turns it on.

He then stands there, leaning, lost in thought.

JOHN *reappears, wiping his mouth with some tissue. He*
watches MARK. MARK *doesn't notice him.*

JOHN. Are you alright?

MARK (*snapping out of it*). Yeah. Are you okay?

JOHN. Yeah, I just. I had a good bit to drink. (*Realising*
MARK*'s demeanour.*) Have you had a few?

MARK. I've had a couple.

JOHN *watches* MARK *making the tea.*

JOHN. You're not very full of Christmas cheer.

MARK *acknowledges this. A snort.*

Do you want a drink?

MARK. Is that alright?

JOHN. Of course it is! Christmas Eve!

MARK. Thanks.

MARK *pours himself a drink.*

Do you want one?

JOHN. Oh Jesus, just give me a small one. Just put a drop in my tea.

MARK *pours a drink for* JOHN *and hands it to him.*

Thanks.

MARK *takes a large slug of whiskey. He doesn't seem used to it.*

Are you alright?

MARK. Yeah.

JOHN. Do you want to maybe put some water in that?

MARK. No, it's okay.

MARK *takes another large slug.*

JOHN. Are you annoyed with me or something?

MARK. What?

JOHN. Are you annoyed at me about your money?

MARK. Ah, no. No.

JOHN. What's wrong with you?

MARK. Nothing. I just didn't have a . . . brilliant afternoon. I'm fine.

JOHN. What happened?

MARK. Nothing.

Pause.

JOHN. Okay.

MARK. Just. When I left here I was going to do something. And I didn't do it, you know?

JOHN. What is it? Do you want me to do it for you?

MARK (*a little laugh*). No. Eh . . . you know Kim. I was telling you . . . earlier.

JOHN. Don't tell me you didn't get her something.

MARK. No. No, no, no.

Pause.

JOHN. What's wrong?

MARK. I just went down to break it off with her, you know?

JOHN. On . . . Christmas Eve?

MARK. No. It's just, she's all on for us to go away together next week. You know? And I don't want to just be making excuses. So I . . . I know it's not a great time. But you know, she's become . . . very intense. About me. And I'm not . . . you know the same.

JOHN. You're not the same about her.

MARK. No.

JOHN. Tch. So you toddled off to tell her.

MARK *nods.*

Down in Marino.

MARK. Yeah.

Pause.

She'd been in work. She started at six or four this morning or something. She was knackered. And I went in to tell her. To her gaff. Her ma let me go up. She was having a lie down.

JOHN (*gives a little laugh*). This is not brilliant.

MARK. I know.

JOHN. What did you say?

MARK (*pause*). Mr Plunkett. (*Beat.*) I don't know. I just was blurting away there. Just her face . . . Just this really faint high-pitched noise started to come out of her.

JOHN. It just couldn't have gone worse. I know. Don't worry about it.

MARK. No . . .

JOHN. She probably has some serious mental disability or something.

MARK. She started sort of grabbing me. And this . . . noise. I was, here, it's okay, it's okay.

JOHN *snorts.*

I thought that like if she was my sister or something. I just stayed there with her. Like no one should . . . (*Cause this much hurt.*) I basically told her I didn't mean it. I've been on my own in the pub across the road for two hours.

MARK *looks at* JOHN.

JOHN. Mm. Well, you know, it might look like you made a bollocks of it.

MARK. Well that's what it feels like.

JOHN. Yeah, but she might've been pulling a sneaky on you, you know?

MARK. No this was, this was real man.

JOHN. Here, give us a drop of that. Give yourself a lash. (*Looks around sharply.*) What time is it?

MARK *pours them both some whiskey.*

Okay, it was real. She had a genuine freak attack, but there's an element of blackmail, in that, do you know what I mean?

Pause.

MARK. That she did it on purpose?

JOHN. She mightn't have done it completely on purpose, but when she felt it coming on, you know? She let the fucking thing fly. You know?

MARK *laughs.*

I'm telling you. You wouldn't be up to them.

MARK. Ah I don't think she'd . . . you know?

JOHN. Yeah but look at it now. Here's you all fretting. You're getting all limbered up to go on a fucking bender. All fucking despair and moaning to your mates on Christmas Eve, all tomorrow wondering if she's gonna eat a bottle of tablets, or end up in Grangegorman, you know? And where's she? She's tucked up in bed, with her mammy filling her full of cup-a-soup and talking about watching *Raiders of the Lost Ark* later on and pulling the couch over to the fire and eating chocolate liquers. Do you see what I mean?

MARK (*laughs*). I just don't think it was on purpose.

JOHN. Look you had a difficult thing to do. You were going down there to tell her the truth. And it was gonna be hard, because I can see by you that you're a sensitive kind of chap, and you were concerned about her feelings. You aren't in the business of dishing out pain and agony and not giving a bollocks. So there you are trying to give the whole thing a bit of respect. It's not like you were doing a bunk with some black girl or hopping on the next train to Timbuctoo. You did the hard thing. And what does she do?

MARK. She might have been still kind of asleep or something though.

JOHN. Yeah but you're upset as well, but you're engaging in it in a grown-up way of sitting down and talking about it. We can all throw fits. We can all lose the head. But that's selfish, though, as well. Because it's mean. It's 'Fuck you. I'm not talking to you.' No acknowledgement that you're trying to do the right thing or nothing, none of that. Just basically, 'Ah you've driven me into the grave, and now you're cursed by the gypsies of County Carlow', you know? It's bollocks.

Pause.

MARK. I should ring her.

JOHN. Nah! Let her ring you. She's probably fucking stalking you now, anyway. She's probably across the road with a pitchfork.

MARK *gives a little laugh.*

Anyway. That's dangerous love. It's different kinds of love
that men and women give. A woman's love can be terribly
constant. Good God. It can last for years! (*Pause.*) There
was this woman loved me unconditionally for many years.
Gave me lifts everywhere. Waited for me. And waited for
me in the long term as well. Waiting on me . . . She was a
widow, you know? And I was still married. I was going into
a nose dive on the booze. It had a real hold of me. She was
very very lonely. Living in a house up there in Sybil Hill.
She was holding down this part time job. Not much money.
She had a little Fiat 127.

She used to drink pots of tea up there in The Beachcomber
in Killester up there. And I'd be skiving off work early,
sneaking around pubs all up in Raheny and Killester and
Harmonstown and then all down here and into town.

Got chatting to her in The Beachcomber. And she hooked
me because she could see that I was very taken with getting
bollocksed and she'd buy me drinks. And it got that I'd . . .
I'd rely on her being in there. This is mad, you know? And
then it was whiskey up in the gaff. (*Pause.*) And I followed
the trail of breadcrumbs all the way into bed. I was more
into the drink than the sex though. She was into neither. She
just couldn't take it on her own. Being on her own. So there
we were. Her loving me and me treating it like a
convenience.

I thought of it like God had sent me like a drink-angel.
Like I believed in God and He'd sent this to take care of
me. And that she was like all confused because she didn't
know why God had sent her. And she didn't know why she
loved me but she just did. God I used to feel sorry for her.
Giving me her last bit of money. Giving me her last fiver
and me asking her if she didn't have any more?! Counting
out her change trying to get it up to the four pints! But that
was the awful disservice I was doing her. The vanity. No it
wasn't vanity. Just that I'd been taught to believe in God!
Poor stupid bitch. You have no idea. You have no idea.

But that was it. I had somewhere to go where I'd get
bollocksed and blot out that I had a, a, a fucking life
somewhere else. So it was easy. And that's dangerous love.
That unconditional, 'I'll do anything to keep you,' fucking
thing. God she had me pickled. You're well shot of this one
and that's the end of it. What are you going to do? Basically
torture yourself until you feel better? You won't feel better
so just . . . bollocks.

Pause.

MARK. Mm.

JOHN. Yeah.

MARK *pours himself a nip of whiskey and pours some into*
JOHN*'s mug.*

MARK. But that's like a fit as well.

JOHN. What?

MARK. You baling off, on your family.

JOHN (*considers*). I'm in a fog.

MARK. Like, you're saying about Kim, that she threw a
freaker and that's . . . not fair on me.

JOHN (*vaguely affirmative*). Uhh.

MARK. You doing a bunk. How is that . . . facing . . . up . . .

JOHN. Well, that's how I know what I'm talking about.

MARK. That's bollocks.

JOHN. What am I supposed to do? Stand here and defend
myself all day?

MARK. Well then don't be dispensing fucking . . . wisdom . . .
I feel like a fucking asshole! You're here telling me what to
do? (*Fiercely.*) I just feel like a fucking eejit!

JOHN. I'm only trying to help you! Why don't you let me
finish?! I'm like the opposite of you . . . What? Am I talking
to you like you're a kid? Is that it?

Pause.

What do you want?

MARK. I'm, look, I'll see you later.

MARK *starts to go.*

JOHN. Don't go like this Mark. It's Christmas.

MARK. Fuck off.

MARK *is leaving.*

JOHN. My wife is dying. I need someone I can talk to, son.

MARK. What?

JOHN. She has cancer in her neck.

Pause.

MARK. This is your wife?

JOHN. Yeah. I haven't seen her for eh, for many years now, you know?

MARK. I'm sorry . . . to hear that.

JOHN. Yeah, well. You know, it's not something I should eh, I should be sympathised with about really. You know?

Silence.

They want me to do her funeral.

Long pause.

What do you think?

MARK. I . . . don't know . . .

JOHN. You're right, you know? About me.

MARK. Look. I don't . . .

JOHN (*slightly too bossy*). Listen to me! (*Apologetic.*) I'm sorry. No. Listen. Listen to me. I'm sorry.

MARK. It's okay. It's alright.

JOHN. My daughter's coming. I don't have much time. She wants me to go to the hospital and see her. I'm just, I really don't know what to do. Your Uncle Noel would know.

Short pause.

MARK. You should go.

JOHN. Yeah?

MARK. You . . . probably should. What if you don't . . . And she . . .

Pause.

JOHN. No. No, you're right. (*Pause. Facing a terrible prospect.*) Paul, he's my . . . son, you know? He's coming home from England. And I haven't seen him since he was eh . . . (*Pause.*) He came around here one time a few years ago. Looking for me. (*He screws up his face a little.*) And I said I wasn't here, you know? They told him I wasn't here. And I just sat over there, waiting until he was gone. And then I changed my mind and went out after him. I just kept going up and down the North Strand looking for him. But, he was gone obviously and that was all there was about it. But I got a letter from him a bit later, telling me he got his Leaving Cert. This is a few years ago. Yeah. What time is it?

MARK. Half four.

JOHN. I better drink some tea.

JOHN *begins to get up.*

MARK. I'll get it.

JOHN *sniffs.*

JOHN. Thanks. Here, you might as well do the advent calendar. We won't be here tomorrow.

MARK *gives a little laugh.*

MARK. Okay.

JOHN. Have a little thrill. Knock yourself out.

MARK *laughs. He opens the last door on the advent calendar.*

What is it?

MARK. It's Jesus.

JOHN. Of course it is. Will you do something for me?

MARK. Yeah.

JOHN. There should be an old box out there in the yard. I want to get the decorations down.

MARK *goes to the door and comes back with a box.*

MARK. I'll give you a hand.

MARK *begins taking things down.*

JOHN. There's nothing worse than decorations after Christmas. That's the way I sometimes used to feel putting my clothes on in the morning.

JOHN *starts helping* MARK. *They work in silence for a while.*

JOHN *regards* MARK *for a moment.*

Don't be worrying. Okay?

MARK. Yeah, I'm . . .

JOHN. I know. You just take it nice and handy now. I think you're probably a born worrier, are you?

MARK. I think I might be.

JOHN. Yeah. Do you know what would be brilliant? For you?

MARK. Yeah?

JOHN. Just to be incredibly fucking thick. Do you know what I mean?

They laugh.

You know?

MARK. Yeah.

JOHN. Yeah . . .

MARK. You're not going to be on your own, are you?
Tomorrow?

JOHN. I don't know. I suppose I was going to be. With Noel
out of action. I was gonna go in and see him, you know?

MARK. We're going in in the morning. Me and Mum.

JOHN. Ah yeah. Good. Yeah I was gonna do that and then,
I don't know. Watch the telly. But. I don't know. To tell you
the truth, I'm not gonna get worked up about it. Tomorrow
is Saturday and that's all. Another filthy morning, only
there's a star in the East. Yeah. Is that it?

MARK. Nearly. The advent calendar.

JOHN. Oh yeah.

JOHN *goes and takes the advent calendar down from the
wall.*

They should have one of these with all year on it.

MARK. Yeah.

JOHN. With little words of wisdom. Little cautionary words of
advice. The second of July. A word of caution. Fourth of
August, a word to the wise. You know? November, 'You're
being a spa, cop on to yourself, you know?'

MARK. A few jokes.

JOHN. A few jokes. Now you're talking. Mister Doom and
Gloom over here. Are you going into town?

MARK. Yeah.

JOHN. You've enough money.

MARK. Yeah, I'm fine. Not gonna be too late anyway.

JOHN. Get into bed before Santa comes and checks.

MARK. And leaves me a bag of soot.

JOHN. Or slips Kim in your stocking.

MARK (*a slightly sad laugh*). Oh fuck.

JOHN. The imagination's gone fucko now.

MARK *has his coat on. He takes out a Walkman and untangles the headphones.*

Oh Walkman! Noel gave me one a few Christmases ago. For sitting outside the church. You couldn't put the radio on in the hearse. It'd be awful, obviously. But you can slip in a little earphone, get the news and that. Yeah, great.

MARK. Yeah.

JOHN. A woman singing in your ear, ha?

MARK *gives a little amused snort. He turns the tape in the machine over.*

Do you have a radio on that?

MARK. Oh yeah. I think there's nearly radios on all of them now.

JOHN. You know if you're listening to the radio and there's all static and you put your hand on it.

MARK. Yeah, you earth it.

JOHN. Yeah and there's a clear signal. It'd be great to be able to do that, wouldn't it? To people, I mean. To people.

Short pause.

MARK. Yeah.

JOHN. Go on. I'm losing the plot. Get outta here. Get out among the living.

MARK. I'll see you on Monday.

JOHN. Yeah there's some poor bastard out there. Looking forward to the old Xmas, not knowing he'll be under this roof on Monday waiting to be buried.

MARK *(a little laugh)*. Could be you or me.

JOHN. Nah . . . *(Gives a little laugh.)* Go on, have a good time.

MARK. Okay.

They shake hands.

Happy Christmas. I'm sorry . . . for your wife.

JOHN. Yeah, Happy Christmas. Thanks. Don't eat too much cake.

MARK. Alright. I'll see you.

MARK *goes.*

JOHN (*calling after him*). And don't be worrying, do you hear me?

MARK (*off*). Yeah, I know.

JOHN *nods. We hear the outer door slam shut.*

JOHN *stands there for a moment and then looks around. He goes and takes a towel from a press and goes to the sink. He pauses and switches on a little transistor radio. Festive music is playing. He takes some soap and washes his face and neck and dries himself briskly.*

He fixes his tie carefully and puts on his jacket and overcoat. Then he takes a comb and does his hair in a little mirror. He is now ready. He stands there collecting himself.

He looks at the box of decorations. He considers them. He goes to the box and takes the advent calendar. He holds it for a moment and decisively places it back on the wall where it was. He returns to the box. He overturns it on the table. He selects some stuff and begins to put the decorations back up. He stands on a chair, redecorating. And from nearby the church bells chime out five o'clock.

The lights begin to fade. Then the music and the bells.

End of Part Three.

PORT AUTHORITY

Port Authority was first produced by the Gate Theatre, Dublin, at the New Ambassadors Theatre, London, on 22 February 2001 and subsequently at the Gate Theatre on 24 April 2001. The cast was as follows:

KEVIN	Éanna MacLiam
DERMOT	Stephen Brennan
JOE	Jim Norton

Director   Conor McPherson
Designer   Eileen Diss
Lighting Designer   Mick Hughes

Characters

KEVIN, *maybe twenty*

DERMOT, *late thirties? mid thirties?*

JOE, *seventy-odd*

Author's Note

The play is set in the theatre.

1

KEVIN

I moved out in the summer.

The house was in Donnycarney and four of us were going to share it.

My folks were not happy about it.

The mad thing was I could see their point.

It was kind of stupid.

I had no job and I didn't know what I wanted to do.

Moving out was like pretending to make a decision.

My dad gave me a lift down to Donnycarney.

With all my clothes in black bin-liners.

It was a bright Sunday afternoon.

I nearly said, 'I'll see you later.'

But this was supposed to be for good.

What a joke.

I was moving in with Davy Rose and a guy called Speedy.

I was mates with Davy.

To everybody else in Dublin he was Mad Davy Rose, hammered on Scrumpy Jack.

But I saw the normal side to him and he spoke to me about stuff and, you know?

Speedy was more Davy's friend than mine.

Although I could hardly see how anyone could be friends with Speedy at all.

He always seemed to me to be unbelievably stupid.

He definitely had a learning disorder or something.

Mostly he was just out of it, but even sober I couldn't make head nor tail of him.

It was like he was excited by being bored.

I had nothing in common with him.

He was asleep in the back garden when I went through.

Davy was sitting in an old deckchair, drinking cider and playing Billy Idol on his ghettoblaster.

He was in a state of agitation because he was in the process of being dumped by this girl with blue hair from Beaumount.

He was all distracted, talking about hopping on his bike going up to annoy her.

I didn't want him to leave me on my own with Speedy so I made him come down to the off-licence with me and I got us more Scrumpy.

And we just went back and kept drinking.

Davy was searching through Speedy's pockets for smokes and I was casually inquiring where Clare was.

She was moving in as well.

Everybody in Dublin was in love with her.

She was buds with me and Davy but she tended to go out with headbangers. Or lads who thought they were, anyway.

She was always with some spiky-haired crusty who you could see was from Dublin 4 or somewhere, putting on a bit of an accent.

They were all rich and spoiled and better looking than any of us.

Davy said he hadn't seen her.

So we got fairly pissed there in the garden and then I went up to see which room was mine.

I had the bedroom at the back.

Davy had the attic conversion.

Clare had the bedroom at the front.

Speedy was in the boxroom.

We were all paying thirty quid, except Speedy who was paying twenty.

All was in my room was a bed and a chair.

I was in my sleeping bag all night lying there awake listening to hear if I could hear Clare come in but all I could hear were all the sounds that made me try to imagine I was still at home.

But it didn't work.

In the morning I borrowed Davy's bike and I went down to Kilbarrack to sign on and sort out rent allowance.

And when I got back it was just Speedy sitting there watching Richard and Judy.

He nodded at me and I sat down there near him.

But he was genuinely watching Richard and Judy.

I was nearly afraid to say anything in case he missed something.

He was eating Rice Krispies like he was on his way out to work in a minute or something.

As if, you know.

And he suddenly starts saying, still not looking at me, about how last Friday a guy from a band from Donaghmede had called down with this small goth girl who was a notorious slut.

And your man was in the back room with Davy jamming on these two bases that were in there.

And your one asks Speedy if he has any hash and he had so they went up to the boxroom and had a spliff and all of a sudden they got stuck into each other, having a sneaky ride.

And Speedy was trying to listen out to hear if he could still
hear your man jamming with Davy and he wasn't coming
up. But your one was starting to make so much noise that
Speedy just got too nervous so he just went into the jacks
and pulled himself off.

And he said all this to me just like that.

And I was just sitting there staring at the side of his head,
thinking that there was nothing he could ever say that could
interest me beyond the terrible notion that I cared absolutely
nothing for this fellow human being. And that if he died I'd
feel nothing.

And we sat there in this room for a while until I could barely
stand it.

Until I casually asked him if he knew when Clare was moving
in.

But there was nothing about Speedy to suggest that anyone had
just spoken to him.

And I was trying to decide whether to ask him again or just
fuck off out or something and he just goes, 'She's here.'

2

DERMOT

Dinner. Friday night. O'Hagan's house.

A kind of a welcome to the fold.

And the elation of a huge salary in an interesting job and
having impressed these clean-shaven tailor-made suits was
clashing with the embarrassment of having to present Mary
to them.

Suddenly I was thinking about my wife.

It was alright when I was at Whelan's.

All the wives looked the same.

Down at the Christmas do in the Old Sheiling.

We moaned about them at the bar.

The way they were squealing at each other.

Hysterical, at being out of the house.

Just a few weeks before I'd been looking for some old accountancy textbooks in the press in the bedroom and a load of chocolate fell out on top of me.

And I just didn't even bother, you know that way?

She took up half the couch and watched *EastEnders*.

And I sat in the boxroom brushing up for the interview.

O'Hagan had rang me himself personally to tell me I'd got it.

Cocktails in Gogarty's Monday night to say hello.

Griffen, Staunton, Crawford. Strong handshakes.

What I presumed was Armani. All ex-rugby.

And then one or two of their wives suddenly.

And I was like, 'Holy fuck, easy Tiger!'

Me in my Penny's blazer and my loafers from Dunnes.

Hardly able, but trying to swallow these Glenmorangies being pressed into my fist.

Swaying in the door.

Mary and Colm curled up in the living room watching *Friends*.

Colm. Nine years of age. Constant cold.

Useless at sports.

Bullied until third class.

Until Mary went down and spoke to the head.

Went down on her own.

Because there was simply only so much I could fit in.

And the head dealt with it.

And I drove Mary and Colm wherever they wanted to go at the
weekends, and although I wouldn't say I was necessarily a
quiet person, I hardly said a fucking word.

Dinner in O'Hagan's house. Friday night.

I whined at Mary about how I needed to dress better.

She took me from shop to shop and I shelled out for three
suits. Cotton shirts. Silk ties.

Catching Mary smiling and seeing what there was to see in her
when we were younger, but we weren't younger now and
I told her that dinner at O'Hagan's was staff only.

No wives. That was another night.

And for once I had something to treasure, that I was looking
forward to.

A glittering jewel on the mountain at the top of Friday.

And me trudging towards it not wanting to get there too
quickly.

Enjoying it in the middle distance.

Because I could see it and it was mine.

And it was going to happen.

3

JOE

Sister Pat knocked while I was getting dressed.

I could smell breakfast being served.

It was the first morning I'd felt hungry in ages.

She had a little box wrapped in brown paper.

It was addressed to me, but at my son's house.

His wife, Lisa, had dropped it in to me on her way to work.

Sister Pat was the closest thing I had to a friend, really.

She was the same age as a lot of the residents but like that old expression, young at heart.

As opposed to me who was just bloody immature.

'It's not your birthday or something, is it?' She says.

'No, my birthday's not 'til June.' I go.

My birthday's not 'til June! Like it'd make a difference!

Sure I hadn't had a birthday present in years, sure!

Who'd be sending an old curmudgeon birthday presents?

And not on his birthday.

I'm not that popular.

Well. I felt like a bit of a twit standing there holding it.

It was very light. But there was definitely something in it.

For a religious, Sister Pat had a lot of little girl in her.

She was being nosy, standing there waiting for me to open it. But, like the bold child she knew she was, she knew I was too awkward to tell her to clear off the hell there out of it.

'Are you not going to open it?' She goes.

'I am.' I say.

Little box covered in brown paper.

Dun Laoghaire postmark.

'I'm going to wait 'til I have my breakfast,' I say.

'And I'll open it when I'm drinking my tea.'

'Do you know what you are?' she says to me, 'You're very vain.'

And she left then.

I knew what she meant, but she said things like that and there was no real anger in it.

And it didn't really make me feel anything really either.

That's just what she was like.

Very direct.

A brilliant nun really.

A perfect bloody nun.

So I put on my jacket and took my stick and I went down the corridor to the dining room.

There was about twenty of us in the home at that point.

Quick look around.

All present and correct.

No one gone up to Beaumont in the middle of the night.

A few of us had sticks.

And a few were in wheelchairs.

But we were fairly agile now, not too bad.

I sat down there beside Jackie Fennel and Mary Larkin.

Who I mostly sat with when I ate.

Often me and Jackie'd wander round to the bookies and get a bottle of stout in Tighe's.

And we'd put little bets on for Mary Larkin as well.

Local women worked in the home and they made you your breakfast and they brought it over to you and everything.

They were great to us.

So there we were and we spoke about the weather and Mary Larkin's son, Peter, who was a guard and whose wife was expecting another baby.

And Jackie Fennel was looking at the racing in the *Independent*.

And now and again I'd think about the little box in my pocket. And my arm'd move a little bit.

And after breakfast when everyone began to mooch off for a chat or do their own thing, I sat there by myself having a cup of tea while the local women cleared up.

And I took out the box and I pulled at the string which I put in my pocket.

And I pulled the paper off neatly because it was all done neatly and I figured out how to get into the cardboard.

And there was a little handwritten note and something flat wrapped in tissue paper.

I pulled it out and I took away the tissue.

It was a small photo that I recognised.

And I knew what had happened and I didn't need to read the note.

4

KEVIN

Clare was sticking luminous stars up on the wall and ceiling of her room.

She wanted to paint the walls.

I said I didn't think we'd be let.

She said this was like a room where you sent your granny to die.

Clare was very much sort of up to the minute.

When you saw her it took you a second but you knew she was special.

She cared about her appearance but in a very discreet way.

She wore make-up but you couldn't see it.

She was definitely sexy but at the same time she was one of the gang and very easy to be with.

For me anyway. And she saw me as like her mate.

Only when you saw her with a lot of other girls was she like . . . a girl.

I was never one of those guys who hung around with a lot of girls, as my friends.

If I knew a girl she was either the girlfriend of someone I knew, or it was someone I was going out with.

So me and Clare was a weird thing for me.

So I was usually thinking about it a lot.

And wondering if . . . you know.

I was putting a plug on her CD player for her and I was looking through her CDs.

She told me to take a tape out of a box beside her bed. It was a demo tape. The guy she was seeing was in a band.

Who wasn't? Everybody I knew was in half-assed bands.

Davy was in The Bangers.

He couldn't really play, but none of those bands were any use.

I'd always have to go into their gigs in pubs in town.

There'd be six bands on, and then like a really drunk band at the end that wasn't really a band, just a mixture of blokes from the other bands and some eejits who were just their mates.

And they'd get up and try and play something by Fugazi or someone, but because it was really hard and no one could really play, they'd have to belt something easy out like 'Anarchy in the UK'.

These were pretty shite gigs now, you know? But I went because all my mates were in that scene and you could have a few beers and a bit of a laugh.

Everybody was a sort of a punk.

This was years after real punk.

But it was like a sub-grouping of people who weren't into Bryan Adams or boy bands and all that.

I wasn't really a punk or anything.

I was just like one of their mates.

Guys like Davy who were notorious as mad bastards all over Dublin. But who I saw the normal side of because we'd grown up together and gone to school together and all that.

Clare's boyfriend's tape was in a case with a photocopied cover in it.

I stuck it in the machine and I was slightly pissed off because they actually sounded quite good.

They sounded like R.E.M. or someone.

'They're really good, aren't they?' Clare goes.

And I had to say yeah, they were.

They'd played support to some quite big bands like The Lemonheads and The Jesus and Mary Chain.

'We should get The Bangers to play with them sometime,' I said.

Clare said yeah. But wasn't like a real yeah, more like . . . yeah! Bit too enthusiastic.

The Bangers were playing that night and we were going in to see them so I went into my room while Clare got ready.

I hadn't unpacked any of my gear. I was pulling all my clothes out but there was nowhere to put them, only on the chair. So I put some trousers on the seat and and some tops on the back, and my trainers underneath.

And I stood back surveying this.

Thinking I had to get much more organised.

But who was I fooling. I was already useless.

Like I was starving and I'd no idea even if there was any food in the house.

I heard the shower go on and I could hear Clare going 'Oh my God!' at the state of the bathroom.

And later on we were down at the bus stop on the Malahide Road.

It was a gorgeous summer's evening.

All amber and a cool breeze.

Clare had one of her runners off shaking a little stone out of it.

I was leaning there looking at the mountains.

And Clare said up to me, she was kneeling on the ground, 'Are you alright?'

And I was looking at the mountains and nodding.

But I didn't think she could see me, so I said, 'Yeah, I'm fine.'

5

DERMOT

Den duh duh.

I was standing on the Dart.

There were plenty of seats but I don't know.

I couldn't sit.

I didn't need to.

All the kids in the latest gear.

Me. Okay older. Okay a bit pudgy.

But none of them had an idea where I was headed.

The windows were black, only a burst of orange in the stations or distant street lamps.

I was watching out for Sutton Cross.

Right there. On my own.

Holding on to a thing. A pole.

And people were getting on, getting off, whatever.

Not too busy because this was the opposite direction to town.
But I was nicely oblivious because I was sort of plunging or
something.

Banging right there into the peninsula from Raheny.

I kept looking up at the map. Like I didn't know.

Mary'd dropped me down to Raheny on her way to a hen
night. And I walked straight over to the station until I saw
her brakelights turn down at the village.

And I was back across over at the boozer like a shot.

Taking my time. Few little G&Ts.

Few little ones in the afternoon as well.

At home while Mary was at the shops.

Before my shower.

Nice form. All the young loolas coming into the pub.

To spend the night here and wobble home, rowing with the
girlfriend.

They could have it.

Three G&Ts later I was down on the platform.

Nicely.

Standing there on the train. Up through Howth Junction.

Bayside.

Bang Bang.

Nearly missed fucking Sutton.

Off I hopped. Straight over to the Marine Hotel, no messing.

Had O'Hagan's address, but I needed a few directions.

Few G&Ts later I felt fully equipped.

You can't ever go off half-cocked, half-medicated into unchartered waters, you'll be eaten alive.

O'Hagan's were one of, if not the most successful money managers in the country. They had all the big musicians and broadcasters and all the big writers and everyone. O'Hagan was a celebrity in his own right.

All the big fashion designers and all.

Christ knew who'd be up at this thing.

So I hung on to his gate for a few minutes snorting up any snot I wanted to get rid of, the sea stretching off towards the lights of the Southside.

And I was veering up his driveway, up to these steps going up to his door, thinking maybe I'd overdone it on the G&Ts, 'cause there'd be plenty of booze inside, and I had this great revelation – that it was too fucking late to do anything about it now!

I didn't even care anymore. So when I found the bell I gave it a right couple of rings to signal my confident arrival.

I was imagining church bells ringing out all across the country. And a little blondie yoke with no straps on her dress and her tits held up with wire opens the door and says, 'Hello!'

'Hello!' I say, lobbing a leg over the threshold and yanking at the sleeve of my anorak.

'Everybody's here,' she says.

'They are now!' says I.

And she doesn't really hear me and she carries my coat off into the house.

And it reminded me of when I was younger and my mum tried to get me into a posh school in Dublin run by the Jesuits. It was all wooden staircases and arched hallways. Did I get in?

Did I fuck!

She hadn't a notion, my mother.

And that's what this house was like.

Only all white. White on the walls and white funny carpet like a tight fishing net.

White little seats everywhere.

And a weird buzzing noise which I realised was people talking to each other.

And the blondie girl gives me champagne no less and brings me into the drawing room while I'm looking at her back.

But I don't know a sinner so I whore away at my glass and there's a tray with more and I take two.

And then 'Dermot!' It's fucking O'Hagan's wife.

Which is okay in itself.

But that she's basically wearing what looks to me like a piece of pink tissue paper and her tits are basically hanging out is giving me a problem.

And it's all see-through, but her tits are basically outside it and she's going 'How are you feeling?'

And I'm like 'Yeah, yeah . . . ' Like I'm cool.

But the controllers in your head who are telling you that you have to live with your future self are filing this moment away under Moronic Moments To Relive Again And Again.

And for some reason I'm thinking about when I was 19 and I used to cycle around on my sister's bike, and my clothes were old. Not old like you Saying Who You Were. But old like you'd had them a few years and the *fibres* were old in them. And they were all a bit grey and even though you didn't, you probably felt like you were probably into little girls. That you felt like you looked like you liked little girls.

And these thoughts were obviously evident in my face so O'Hagan's wife is saying 'Don't be intimidated!'

And she takes my arm and starts saying, 'Come on, we're all going to eat now.' And she's pulling me along and I feel like I'm going to go over on my snot so I'm walking all funny.

And then all of a sud we're going down a spiral staircase.

And then we're at the bottom and I'm like 'How the fuck did I manage that?' And sort of congratulating myself and I hear all this 'Dermot!' 'Dermot!' 'Over here!'

And there they all are. O'Hagan, Crawford, Staunton, all sitting down to eat rabbits while a woman like my mum is putting roast 'dates* down in a big flat bowl.

And Crawford is saying something like 'Dermot, don't ever be afraid of roast potatoes,' or something.

And I go, 'What the fuck are you saying?'

But nobody hears me.

And I feel a row coming on, but I'm on top of it.

And I think that I'll probably just break something later instead.

And the little blondie one seems to be in charge of everything.

But like she's been hired, at the same time she's like everyone's friend. And they all call her Charlotte and so do I because she's pumping the wine into everybody and constantly opening bottles.

And I realise that all the women at the table are like what I see in Mary's magazines.

All dressed like they always are, just before it all has to come off. Because it just has to.

And I'm watching Charlotte's severe fringe and the freckles across her nose and her tan and O'Hagan's wife plonks down right opposite me.

And I try to distract myself by working out if we're on benches or seats, but if I check I'm a goner.

So I just silently place my hands on the table.

My head is the moon and I've got to keep it away from the earth.

I use my arms to do this.

* *Potatoes.*

And I use O'Hagan's wife's mostly visible tits to keep the astronauts from panicking.

We panic and we're gone.

So we're using O'Hagan's wife's tits as a vital NASA supply to balance our brains. Because we can, in our distraction, act automatically, and just use our reflexes, which are nature's cause and effect certainties.

And slowly I notice that everything has gone very quiet.

And I hear someone say 'Dermot?'

And I realise that someone must have just asked me a question.

And everyone's just twigged why the fuck I can't answer.

And O'Hagan's wife has a big reddener and she's got her napkin practically up at her neck.

And I have this overwhelming urge to use the toilet.

And not just use the toilet.

Use the fact that it has walls.

And that no one has X-ray eyes.

But of course they do, don't they?

Of course they fucking do.

6

JOE

I'm going to tell you something, right?

I was always just like everybody else.

Do you get me?

There was simply never any question about it.

You saw me with a bunch of people, you wouldn't notice me.

I never thought about myself.

I saw the world as a very organised place that was easy to negotiate. I saw people as generally good and if there were blackguards around the place - well that's what they were. Blackguards.

I met my wife, Liz, when I was working up in Cadbury's.

I was older than her and I'd sort of risen up through the ranks a bit by then and she was working on the floor.

Which made it a bit difficult to bump into her.

But I always had my eye on her. Don't know why.

She had thick little legs. She was small and a bit . . . busty I suppose.

Got my chance to ask her up at the Christmas dance 1956.

To my astonishment she had no boyfriend and we started going out together.

I had a pretty flash car, an Austin, and I was still living with the parentals, so I had a few bob.

And Liz was basically a smasher in many ways.

Always laughing. Always in good form.

If there was an awkward silence, she just hummed to herself. Do you get me?

She was like me.

There was nothing neither wrong nor right about us.

I could easily stand in her parents' living room at Christmas time and she could easily sit in mine.

We got married in Cabra in 1960 and moved into a house in Donnycarney.

In those days in Ireland like, you didn't have a lot of the issues that you do now.

She cooked the dinner and packed in the job and I earned the spons. That was it. There was none of your everyone's on valium because they're all confused about who they are.

Listen, I'm not saying that things were better then than now, only different and you didn't need to be asking all the questions you do now. And to tell you the truth that suited me. That suited me down to the ground. Because when the time came for me to have to start asking questions, let me tell you at the time, I could've done without it.

Or maybe I'm glad it happened.

You see? I've no idea about myself!

I don't even know if I'm happy or sad!

But how and ever. Liz became pregnant with Stephen in '61. And two years later we had Tania.

Not a family name. Liz saw it in a film.

Oh, the times they were a changing, for sure.

And after a few years and the kids were that bit older and I was still earning a nice few bob, we decided to move to a bigger house.

A beautiful house up in Sutton.

Right there on the peninsula.

7

KEVIN

It was an absolutely dismal night for The Bangers.

It was the first time they'd headlined their own gig.

So they were paying for the rent on the venue and they'd had to hire the P.A.

There were supposed to be three bands, one of who, The Lepers, had a big following on their own.

But they'd had to cancel because one of them had lost a finger in the sheet metal factory where he worked.

Yeah, yeah, the jokes about the leper who'd lost his finger were endless.

A completely brutal band from Skerries were on.

It was ten o'clock and there were only about fifteen people in the place.

Davy was just getting hammered on Scrumpy Jack.

He had a bag of cans under the table.

He was talking about not going on.

Scampi, The Bangers' lead singer was saying they might as well now they were here. Their guitar player Vinnie Harper said he couldn't give a shit either way.

Danny the drummer had shifted this small goth chick so he wasn't going anywhere.

It was lashing rain outside and the whole thing was just generally a bit depressing.

I was embarrassed for them as well because Clare had managed to drag her boyfriend along.

Not only was he a proper musician and actually worked, he had a job in a printers, he was actually a nice guy.

His name was Declan. Into that whole suede jacket, jeans and boots vibe.

Big sideburns on him.

And because Clare usually went out with terrible fucking morons I reckoned this might be the real thing.

She wasn't all over him or anything.

You could just tell she was into him.

Whenever he said anything, well you had to shout really at those gigs, she was right in there. Leaning in.

Giving him her ear. Nodding. Following him. Getting it, you know?

I was beginning to feel sick of the whole not-living-with-your-folks thing.

Clare couldn't stand Speedy. He was just constantly out of it. He was filthy and he always ate all her food.

It was a bad atmosphere.

Davy's genius solution was to have a big housewarming party to clear the air.

Without asking any of us he'd printed up flyers and fucking everyone in Dublin seemed to have one.

There was still two weeks to go and the word of mouth was becoming enormous.

I was seriously thinking about moving back home because basically it was going to be mental, the neighbours would definitely be calling the guards and the landlord who was a bit of a cunt anyway would have us all out on our snot in a heartbeat.

So there I was on this disastrous night for The Bangers and I was more or less lost in thought.

Davy had finally been persuaded to go on.

Vinnie Harper was only starting to tune up his guitar but Scampi just shouts 'We're The Bangers!'

And Davy just sort of jumped into the drumkit and they were away.

A couple of drunk crusties started moshing around a bit, but the truth was I'd never heard them sound worse.

Clare's boyfriend sat there with a stunned look of morbid interest. And me and Clare just looked at each other and burst out laughing. And I just went (*Mimes lifting glass to his mouth.*) And she goes (*Thumbs-up sign.*)

So I wandered off downstairs to the empty bar.

Only little old men drank in here and it was dead.

I stood there staring up at an old photo of some priests holding
up a big cheque and someone slapped me lightly across the
face.

It was the girl working behind the counter.

She was my age and she had lots of curly hair.

'Wakey wakey,' she goes.

I snapped out of it and asked her for two pints of Bulmers.

'You upstairs?' she asks me, sort of looking at me.

'Yeah,' I said. 'It's fucking awful.'

And later on I was sitting in Jimmy Dean's diner with Clare
and her boyfriend. And Davy was getting sick in the jacks.

And the barmaid who'd slapped me, whose name was Trish
came in and joined us.

And I wasn't completely surprised.

Because when I'd asked her to she said she definitely might
alright.

8

DERMOT

Don't ever try to work anything out.

Because you don't know – and you never will.

And even if you do, it'll be too late to do anything about it
anyway.

Just don't bother. You'd think I'd been a disaster at O'Hagan's
party?

A danger to shipping?

An embarrassment at the very least, ha?

A tableful of people had just watched me transfixed, I mean transported by my bosses wife's boobs.

A tableful of whatdoyoucallit, your colleagues.

But nothing was normal about this.

Are you normal?

'Cause if you think you are – you'll be like me.

Sitting on the toilet.

Clenching my fists and unclenching them.

Rocking back and forth.

Staring into the fact that I'd blown it.

Blown it all to hell up the wazoo.

Trying to ignore the little knocks at the door.

No one was going to throw me out. I'd leave of my own accord when I was good and ready, clutching the last shreds of my dignity on my own, thank you very much.

But it was the way O'Hagan's wife said my name.

'Dermot?' she said. 'Are you alright?'

The way she said it.

Through the door.

There was no punishment in it.

No judgement or something.

Unbelievably.

It made me open the door.

So I stood there and I started to say how sorry I was and too much to drink and so on.

But she just laughed a little sad laugh.

And placed a reassuring hand on my arm.

And I heard O'Hagan and the others shouting from the kitchen.

'Dermo!' O'Hagan was going. 'Get yourself back in here and have your sweet, you fucking eejit!'

And I went back in there with his wife.

What is it? Money? Or Royalty or something?

Where the rules are different.

But I should have twigged that something was weird about all this ages before.

Right there in the beginning.

At the interview.

I mean, I don't think they even asked me about three questions. Three maybe. And they were like general 'what do you make of the present state of affairs as they stand at the moment' type questions.

Rhetorical, even, like, 'Who can say what way the bloody country is going, ha?'

I mean, how do you answer?

You know?

You sort of go, 'Well, it's very hard to say, isn't it?' That's all I could do.   ·

And O'Hagan just goes, 'Well everything we've heard about you is very impressive, and we'll be in touch.'

Heard what about me?

That I'd never actually passed my ACCA?

Or that in the eighteen months I'd worked in Denis Mahony's I never sold a single car? Not one!

Or what, that I'd been sacked out of Whelan's for so-called sexual harrassment? Of, supposedly, another man!

What? That I was just generally a bit of a disaster?

Whatever they'd heard, I wasn't going to question it!

They'd given me the job and here I was.

I mean I sat back down there at the table and I was *totally* accepted.

And I hadn't even started working yet, you know?

Well, what the fuck.

Here were coming the cigars and I took one and someone else's wife lit it for me.

And O'Hagan comes down beside me.

His big arm around my shoulders.

'You're a man after my own heart,' he goes, 'Ha? Ha?'

Me smiling and nodding, pretending I know what the fuck is going on.

And then he goes 'You ever heard of The Bangers?'

Had I what?

They were the biggest thing out of Ireland since The Cranberries. They were going to be as big as U2.

Huge in the States.

'We look after them,' he says, 'They're kicking off their tour in Los Angeles St Patrick's weekend. We're all going to go. Are you free?' He says to me.

Well it was that or round to Mary's mother's house for corned beef and cabbage and rock hard potatoes.

So I thought about it.

For about a millisecond.

The big blank head on me.

9

JOE

You want a tip?

When you dream in the night, just wake up, forget about it, get on with it, get up in the morning and have your breakfast and go to work.

Be courteous in your job and use your manners.

'Cause if you dream that someone's loving you and you wake up looking for them and sending signals to all and sundry around you in the daytime, saying was it you? Was it you who loved me?

You'll fucking find them, mark my words.

They'll come to you.

They'll seem different.

Like someone who's changed over the years like you knew them as a child. But it'll be them.

And all that longing that's in you.

When you thought you'd never meet again and a dam bursts.

It's all in you.

And for an ordinary man like me to discover that.

Well it was slightly the end of the world there for a little while.

What happened was this.

When we moved up to the peninsula, up to Sutton, our nextdoor neighbours invited us into a party in their house one Saturday night.

His name was Tommy Ross and his wife's name was Marion.

They were having a family do.

It was Tommy's parents' anniversary and they were throwing a bit of a bash.

I'd only ever chatted to him a little bit maybe in the garden in the morning. I'd never spoken to her.

Liz, my wife, had tended to stay friendly with her old pals from Cadbury's and from where we'd lived in Donnycarney.

Stephen was ten and Tania was eight.

Naturally, they fought like tigers, so even though we were only going next door for a few hours Liz's sister, Aunty Carmel, came up to babysit and we were able to go.

And even though we didn't know anyone at all, you see in those days you just spoke to people.

Even though then it was like it is now and people had a few bob.

We'd bought a table set for Tom's parents and we chatted to them for a while.

And I spoke to one of Tom's brothers, Frank and his wife, Phyllis and Liz was chatting to another sister, Bernie.

And it was all very pleasant.

In those days I drank bottles of Smithwicks.

And there was all six-packs of Smithwicks and Guinness and Harp all stacked up in the garage, and all the nieces and nephews'd bring some in and take out the empties and all this and it was about ten o'clock and very pleasant.

The first one or two early risers might have started to leave, but things were more or less in full swing.

And I went into the kitchen at one point to get myself another ham sandwich or an egg sandwich and I got talking to Tom Ross's wife, Marion, and as we'd never really spoken before, it was only natural that we should fill in a lot of history, being new neighbours.

Now before you start thinking, 'Yo ho! Here's where it gets good!' let me explain that there were other people in the kitchen and this was all normal and acceptable.

Only, the night before I'd had a dream that I was down at this
river and there was a woman there with jet black hair and
the unconditional no-nonsense acceptance I'd felt was like,
when I woke up, that I'd lost a part of myself.

Not that Marion looked anything like this woman in the dream.

She looked nothing like her.

She had short fair hair and a little pug nose.

And she was telling me about the people who'd lived next door
before we moved in and how horrible they were, and I was
just staring at her for some reason and the strange way she
twisted her jaw when she became full of good-humoured
bad thoughts about people she was criticising.

And I was desperately trying to cop onto myself.

And eat this bloody ham sandwich, but there was no water in
my mouth so I was drinking too much Smithwicks.

But it all seemed so bloody unimportant when I watched her
little leg spin whenever she heard a song she liked come on.

So I made sure we made our way out to the living room and I
stood there with my arm on Liz for the rest of the night.

With everyone, including Marion, oblivious of what had just
happened to me.

And me putting it all out of my mind hopelessly as a passing
nonsense that'd do nobody any good in the long run.

And you fool yourself that God hasn't seen you.

But there were a few little involuntary twitches in my legs and
hands for the next hour or two until we went to bed, let me
tell you!

. . . I put it down to the drink.

And of course to that bloody dream I'd had.

And that was the end of that.

But, of course it was impossible for Him not to, God had seen
me.

10

KEVIN

I had a comfortable time then.

Trish was a student at NCAD.

And she worked in the pub in the evenings.

I was like a little old man there.

Going in. Sitting up there watching the snooker.

Having a pint or two.

She lived around the corner in a flat on Parliament Street.

We fucked all night all the time.

She'd shake her head, all her curly hair hitting me in the face.

All her pent-up frustrations about being from the country.

Her legs around mine so I couldn't get away.

The condom coming off and bursting and every fucking thing.

She didn't speak to me much though.

Not about anything important.

You even looked at her too long, I mean admiringly, she'd come straight over and punch you in the chest, wanting to know what you were staring at.

But other things like, you'd be standing there in the Spar buying a can of Coke and her hand would slip into mine, absent-mindedly, and automatic, no strings attached, just proper love.

The light blazing across her face when we were sitting on the bus, upstairs at the front.

Going out through Fairview up to Donnycarney.

She loved Davy.

They were the same.

They wanted more than the world had to give them.

She drank and dragged me to my feet to dance, her hand clamped on my arse.

Clare was confused by her a bit I think.

And, maybe it was because, all of a sud, here was something me and Clare couldn't talk about.

All of us there hanging round the house.

Clare giving Davy a hard time about the whole of Dublin being invited to the housewarming.

Davy in a stupor.

Speedy mostly asleep.

I was watching *The Simpsons* and I got up to make a cup of coffee.

And Trish and Clare were standing there in the kitchen talking and I moved between them like I wasn't welcome.

Like I needed a friend.

And we went down to the pub and Trish got up to get a round and I was eating some crisps and I caught Clare looking at me and we started laughing.

Well it was that or bursting into tears or some fucking thing.

Later on in the chipper Clare began to get organised about we had to go to the supermarket the next day because if Davy wasn't going to do anything about this party, then we had to.

Trish was pretending her battered sausage was someone's dick. She only had a grey vest top on.

And later on she gave me the most unbelievable blow job.

I nearly came all over the place.

You see someone laughing with your spunk all over them, let's face it, you're on to a good thing.

All in her curly hair and all.

And that night we fell asleep together for the first time.

She was late for college and everything.

I had my jeans on and I was eating cornflakes there in my bare feet and Clare comes into the kitchen twirling car keys on her finger.

She'd borrowed her mam's Fiesta.

And we drove down to Superquinn in Sutton Cross.

She had a silver bracelet on her left arm and she had a tan and I was watching it when she changed gears.

And projecting ahead like we were married and this was what we did all the time.

The little concentrated look on her face going up through the traffic.

Her thin lips at all the bad drivers.

And I'd never done anything like this except with my mum, pushing a trolley around the supermarket.

I just wanted to grab Clare right there.

She had sporty stripes down her pants.

She had no socks on.

And just, her stupid ankles there.

Like she'd never need to wear socks if she was with me or something.

Obviously I was losing it, so I clamped my fingers around the handle on the trolley.

And we both knew this housewarming thing was going to be disastrous.

And I began to realise that Clare had to know there was no point in buying stuff for a bunch of mentlers who were going to come and just basically drink you out of house and home.

And I knew that all this supermarket bullshit was because
Clare just wanted to spend some time with me again.

And she turned at one point and put her hand on my belly
while we were looking at frozen pizzas.

And for ages we couldn't move.

11

DERMOT

First class on a plane?

To America?

It's all napkins and tablecloths and 'You were drinking the
Chardonnay, sir?'

It's stupid.

I don't know how much it costs, but we're talking thousands,
yeah?

And it was St Patrick's weekend, so they were all there.

Adams, McGuinness, Reynolds, Cowan, Ahern, Eammon
Dunphy, Ian Dempsey, and me, and O'Hagan, and Crawford
Griffen, Staunton, and all their wives.

But no Mary.

She'd stood there in the shadow and the light there on the
landing, my hand on hers on the bannister.

'I have to go,' I said, 'They're making me.'

And fuck, she saw right through me.

She didn't say a fucking word.

But she'd clocked me.

I was snared.

But where do you go?

You stay where you are.

And she nodded and smiled and went off into the bathroom.

And I used the sound of the bath running to open the drinks cabinet and help myself to some strange cocktail which kicked in a little while later while I was lying on the sofa thinking about LA.

And here I was!

On the broom-broom.

And we're all getting up and walking around like we're in a club or something.

Meeting and greeting. Pressing the flesh.

With the great and the good.

The air hostesses all licking up to us, everybody laughing at everybody else's stupid comments.

But nothing could hide that there was a bit of a smell of shit on the plane, like one of the jacks was broken or something.

A smell to which I have to say I contributed to with a couple of hefty pounds of crap myself.

It goes in, it comes out!

What are you going to do? Hold it in?

I stank up my bloody hotel room first thing as well.

We'd all been picked up by limos.

I was knackered and fairly drunk from the plane.

And The Banger's concert was that night.

'Don't go asleep, Dermot,' they were all warning me.

'The only way to beat the jet lag is to stay up.'

Stay up! I felt like it was half eleven at night and I'd been in the pub all day.

Stay up . . .

I sat there on the bed in the hotel.

I had a load of rooms. One like a sitting room.

One for like having your nosh or to hold a meeting in. And one like a proper hotel room with a bed. Me in the middle. The stinky smell of my crap all over the place.

Mary'd packed this pair of shorts she'd got me.

They were like cool combat shorts with big pockets on the side of them.

So I put them on and went down looking for the bar.

But at reception they told me the bar didn't open until like six or something ridiculous.

So I wandered back up to my room and I sat on the balcony looking down into the empty pool, and I made a right few dents into the minibar until the phone finally rang and it was time to go down to the lobby where we were all meeting our limo to take us to see The Bangers.

But in truth we weren't going to see The Bangers.

We were going to The Banger's concert which is different.

We were going to be backstage in the VIP enclosure.

All O'Hagan and them and their wives all dressed casual, all hip and laid back and not millionaires, all in their brand new sparkling white Nikes.

So if you said to me, 'What are The Bangers like live?' I couldn't tell you.

But I can tell you that backstage is like something out of *Lord of the Rings.*

You can see the stage and the speakers towering up and all banners blowing in the wind like a castle and a little village of people all milling around. All hoping that some rubbish is going to be thrown out of the castle one day, and by mistake there'll be something good in it, like a diamond, and if you're the one that finds it you're never going to have to work again or ever be hungry anymore.

I was beginning to feel scared and the night air was cold and I was trying to numb all my fears by drinking vodka. And I got talking to some blonde girl and her husband. He was English and on the off-chance that I was someone important they were being very friendly towards me. And they asked me if I wanted to take some cocaine.

I'd never taken it in my life but I wanted anything to take away these scary feelings I was having.

So we snorted this cocaine up our noses in a portaloo.

The smell of shit was overwhelming and a roar went up from eighty thousand people and I spun out into the night, quite convinced that bats were going to attack me.

And I had a bottle of vodka in my hand and I cowered in the corner of a field, feeling that my life was in great danger.

Until O'Hagan's wife found me and we went to some party where I couldn't stay and the next thing I knew I was back in the hotel room.

It had started to get bright.

I had my shorts on and I was looking at the weird dimples on this girl's breast implants where it looked all plastic.

And I was on the phone and I was talking to Mary.

She was down there in Artane at her parents' house on the estate. She was on her mobile and nieces and nephews were arriving for St Patrick's Day.

I could hear them squealing.

She was standing there in the garden and I could imagine it.

All the sounds were all so innocent and somehow very real. There was an echo which struck me as something to do with the summer and I couldn't take it any more so I said, 'Take it easy.' And I put the phone down.

And this girl on the bed was asleep and I was looking at her vagina and wondering how old she was and who she was, it was a plump dark line, and I was wondering if this funny feeling of the carpet under my feet was a feeling of remorse.

And I began to go asleep and the sun was beginning to shriek in the windows.

And then later, O'Hagan was in the room and the girl seemed to have gone.

And we were slowly playing with the minibar like it was a minibar on the Titanic and we were divers from some crazy museum.

And he told me that someone had made a terrible mistake.

Someone had recommended someone with the same name as me to Crawford. Someone at his rugby club.

And they'd made the mistake of giving me the job.

Because they saw my CV first.

But I knew something like this was bound to happen.

He was apologising, saying it was a monumental cock-up.

And he'd only just found out.

But he eyed me steadily while he told me that if I did anything stupid like trying to sue him, the minute I met his lawyers I'd be dead in the water.

And I hadn't a chance.

I waved my hand limply.

We were both really out of it.

And he kept saying, 'Good man. Good man.'

And I'd be reimbursed for my inconvenience.

It was just that they'd thought I was somebody else.

He stood at the wall.

And his wife kept ringing the room to see if he was ready to go out for dinner.

And he told me his mother had died a few months ago and she wanted, in her will, for some photo of herself to be sent to some man who used to be their next-door neighbour.

He couldn't rest any more, he said, thinking about it.

'But I suppose,' he said, 'The past is over, isn't it?'

Later on they were all gone out to dinner and I was on the phone, trying to find out how I could fly back to Dublin.

But I can't remember too much of all this, understandably, because it was all very much like some dream I was having.

There's no way of saying it even without it all seeming very strange to me.

But, like O'Hagan says, the past is over.

Isn't it?

12

JOE

In those days a lot of us could just about boil an egg. Those of us who worked a lot.

There just wasn't the time.

There just wasn't the need.

Breakfast with the kids.

Soup and sandwiches at your lunch.

And off home to your shepherd's pie or your few chops for your tea. Sure you spent half your time trying to get it into the kids, any way you could.

So when they found a cyst on one of Liz's ovaries and the date was set for her to go in and have it done, it was decided that Dermot and Tania would stay with

Liz's sister Aunty Carmel in Baldoyle.

We drove Liz up to the Bons on a Sunday.

We went into her little room and the kids sat on the bed while she took her few bits out of her overnight bag and got into her nightie.

And pretty soon the sister came in to say the specialist was on his way.

So we all gave Liz a kiss and I drove the kids up to Baldoyle.

Aunty Carmel gave us some mushroom omelettes and chips.

And when I left them there, there were no tears or no messing.

This was an adventure for the kids there with their cousins.

Sleeping in their cousins' beds and everything.

And I went home and ran a bath.

I'd barely seen Marion or Tommy Ross since their party.

Which was probably a mistake in itself though.

Because, because I'd gotten a land for myself that night in the kitchen with Marion, and if you don't see the person and see all their little ways that make them normal, you sort of, involuntarily romanticise them, don't you?

It was like the next-door neighbours' house was like some kind of bizarre memorial or something.

To what, I don't know.

Some strange dream or the constant possibility that you can get yourself a bit of a land for yourself, maybe.

And our house felt fierce empty in the morning.

And I phoned Aunty Carmel and spoke to the kids and ate some bread and butter and tea.

And you know the way sometimes you go to work, but everything's different and there's a calmness in you that you didn't think it was possible for you to have?

A strange floaty day.

I suppose because your normal routine is that bit upset.

I left a little early and went up to the Bons where Liz was fasting.

She was in good form and more looking forward to getting it over with than afraid.

She was a real Dublin spirit.

And I spoke to the specialist, Mr Ellis, and we were all very businesslike all of a sudden, but it was time to go and I dropped a load of chocolate off up to Aunty Carmel's for the kids and the cousins.

But they were all out the back playing on a swing they'd made from one of the trees, and they hardly paid me any notice so I drove off home.

And there I was, sitting there watching the news and thinking about maybe opening a tin of beans or maybe nipping out for a fish and chip, when perhaps you might say inevitably, the door bell rang, and there was Marion with a plateful of dinner with tinfoil over it.

Which, of course, as a Christian you have to appreciate but because as well this person has reached mythic proportions in your sense of what's right and wrong and what can tip the balance into some kind of unpredictable insanity you take the plate with slight trepidation, don't you?

But of course she was completely innocent of anything as, technically, we both were.

And she actually stood at the sink and did my breakfast dishes while I ate this food that was very alien to me and I didn't quite know what it was.

And she was inquiring after Liz and how we were all coping.

And I was trying to work out if she'd done anything to her appearance before dropping in.

Anything to make herself in any way more appealing than she otherwise might've needed to.

And I was sitting there, deciding she hadn't, she was wearing Scholl sandals and a scarf on her head.

And she suddenly stopped and said, 'Is that Bay Rum?' which was something I usually used in my hair in those days.

I said, yes, it was.

And she was slightly miles away like the smell or me or both or whatever, reminded her of something.

And before she left she said she'd keep an eye on me and if there was anything I needed done, washing or anything, just to give her a shout.

And why I felt so bad without having done or said anything bad, it was awful.

And I was afraid of my life that I'd be punished somehow by Liz's operation going awry in some way or that God was telling me He was taking her away because I was really supposed to be with somebody else.

But, she was fine and clean as a whistle when I went in to see her the next evening and Mr Ellis was confident she'd be home within the week.

Which I took as a sign that everything was alright and normal in the world and not to be giving myself heart attacks over nothing.

But it was a fine, bright April evening and Marion and Tommy Ross called in to see how Liz was getting on and did I want my dinner.

They had a little white dog with them on a leash and they were going for a walk and asked me if I'd like to join them but I felt so full of loss looking at Marion pulling at the dog's leash that I had to say no.

And Tommy told me to call into them for a nightcap later and I said I would because I needed to get the door shut so I could lean against the wall.

With like this image of Marion looking down at the little dog and pulling at the leash, her elbow going up, emblazoned into my eyes or something.

And I sat on the stairs and actually watched the house get dark before I got up and went next door.

For a nightcap.

Tommy brought me in and we chatted about various things, like work and politics.

And Marion was upstairs with one of the kids who was getting a bit of a temperature.

But she soon came down and had a Bacardi and Coke with us and I was about to push off, because I felt I needed a few stiffeners at home to sort myself out.

And their little boy came down and he wasn't well and Tommy brought him back up and Marion went to see if she had the number of the doctor.

And for a minute I was alone there in their living room and I was staring at a bookcase and I saw this black-and-white picture of Marion when she was like only a child. But she looked exactly the same.

And she was grinning into the camera with a look halfway between innocence and a dawning mischief that there were things in the world you could get away with.

And I picked it up and I tried to put it in my pocket.

And Marion came back in and basically she caught me.

I pretended I was just wiping it on my jacket, like it was a bit dusty or something.

And I was sort of going 'Is this you? Ha ha ha.'

But she had a cold serious look in her eyes and she just said to me, 'Do you want that?'

And I was like, 'What? Are you mad? What do you mean? Ha ha ha.'

But she was just 'Do you want that?'

And I didn't know what to say.

And she said, 'You can have it if you want it.'

She said, 'You can keep that. If you want it.'

And she was so calm about it in a way that I couldn't
understand that I nearly did. I nearly took it.

But of course all your dead relatives and teachers from your
youth and all the things that are basically yourself are all
there, aghast, and I just put it back on the bookcase.

And I went towards the door which meant that I went past her
brown shoulder and out into the garden and back into my
house where I lay curled up on the sofa, half expecting a
soft knocking at the front door or the window which never
came.

And I knew that I couldn't take that photograph because I was
afraid to. And I was afraid to because I didn't know why I
wanted it.

And I felt like that was the truth.

And I barely ever saw or spoke to that woman again.

For better or for worse. Or both, mmm?

Because that's what you do.

13

KEVIN

Predictably by about one o'clock in the morning panes of glass
were broken in the living-room door.

The guards had already been once to tell us to keep the racket
down.

An ambulance had been because some poor eejit had gotten a
hiding on his way to the party and he arrived with his nose
all over his face.

There was another fight brewing in the front garden between
the local hardchaws and a load of crusties who hung out in
town.

They were fucking beer cans at each other across the street.

Speedy had fallen asleep in the toilet and the door was locked. Davy finally had to kick it in so the girls could have somewhere to have a slash.

The boys were all just doing it in the garden.

The smell of cider piss out the back was all over the neighbourhood. It was like vinegar and the grass was all dead.

There was just a mad atmosphere.

Davy opened up his plastic dustbin full of homebrew.

It was supposed to ferment for two months.

But he'd only started making it on Tuesday and everyone was milling it.

Someone's dad was at the party, standing in the hall, calm as you like, drinking a can of Royal Dutch and talking to this really boring American guy who always seemed to turn up everywhere.

A girl fell down the stairs and people were saying we were going to have to call another ambulance.

And even though me and Clare had locked our bedroom doors there were people in them, and it wasn't worth the hassle trying to get them out.

We were all past caring.

I was standing in the back garden.

Someone had just handed me a goldfish in a little plastic bag full of water.

Unbelievably it was still alive.

No one knew where it came from.

There'd nearly been a mill when one of Clare's old flames had tried to headbutt Declan, her new boyfriend.

But it was over pretty quickly with Clare tearing into your man, screaming insults into his face until he just stood on his own over at the kitchen door, hanging his head in an unbelievable wave of shame.

A little while before I'd seen Trish's curly hair under the oil tank. She was snogging this guy in a big woolly hat. And then she stood up and turned and saw me and I totally believed her as she staggered away saying, 'I thought that was you!', her hands up to her face, starting to laugh.

The chap under the oil tank reached up to her and let out an indistinguishable 'Ughhh . . . ' protesting to her. And she just turned and gave him the most almighty kick in the face I've ever seen. He was too drunk to feel it and he was asleep immediately.

It was that type of atmosphere.

Scampi had pulled Davy's amp out into the garden and he was trying to persuade The Bangers to crank up and do a few songs.

And suddenly a football appeared and there was an impromptu game in full swing with no teams and no goalposts, just loads of random boots and people running around with a mad sense of purpose.

I went over to the side of the house and stood in the passage to protect the little fish.

I kicked some full cans of Scrumpy in the darkness and I started to drink them.

Some girl tried to snog me for a minute but I was rapidly becoming just generally incapable.

And someone ran up to me and said 'Paul McCartney's actually here!'

And I suddenly felt like there was just nowhere to go.

And the police arrived again and soon it was all over.

Davy was nearly arrested only Clare intervened on his behalf saying he was mentally ill.

And I just basically stayed up in the garden all night wandering around drinking from various cans that were scattered about.

And when it was bright I went up to my room to have a sleep but there were people there already.

So I tapped on Clare's door and went in.

She lay on her side, her eyes were open.

Declan was asleep with his arm round her.

I sat down beside the bed with her looking at me.

And I gave her a look that said, 'Well, that's that.'

And she smiled and she slowly got up to put some clothes on, her brown skin shining in the morning light.

And went downstairs, not saying anything and we went for a walk.

We walked down the Malahide Road, down to Fairview.

Down the Alfie Byrne Road, down past Sheriff Street, down by the Point and across the toll bridge, down to Ringsend.

Down through Sandymount, on out past Booterstown, into Blackrock, down through Monkstown and out into Dun Laoghaire where we walked out onto the harbour wall.

I looked into the bag but the fish had died.

And we walked down the harbour in silence.

Sometimes Clare seemed to take my hand like maybe she wanted to go back.

But I kept going. And she stayed with me.

We'd have to go back soon anyway.

We were running out of land to walk on.

It was just miles and miles of sea.

There was just nowhere left to go anymore.

Except just sort of towards each other for a while.

'What did I say?' My dad said.

'What did I say?'

I was tucking into a bit of Sunday dinner.

'I give it a month! That's what I said. What did I say?'

And to tell you the truth I didn't mind him having his little moment of triumph.

It was a relief, back home, with my mum and dad and my sisters.

My room was just as I'd left it, only tidy, and with clean sheets. And I slept for fifteen hours that night.

And a few nights later Clare called down and we sat in the kitchen drinking cups of tea, listening to the radio.

She was going mad, she said. Back with the folks.

All evening about how it was doing her head in.

But I knew where it was all going.

She was moving out into another house.

With Declan and some of his mates in their band.

And I was sitting there, telling her that this was a great idea.

And there was just something stopping us talking about each other properly. To each other.

Fear? Bewilderment? Disbelief maybe?

That this couldn't be it.

That two people couldn't have found each other this easily.

We didn't trust it I suppose.

So that was that.

And we soldiered on off down our different roads.

A few weeks later my granny died.

My dad's mum.

And I was sitting there at the funeral, watching my granddad holding these rosary beads that had belonged to her, that she'd got from Lourdes.

And I was thinking that maybe there isn't a soul for every person in the world.

Maybe there's just two.

One for people who go with the flow, and one for all the people who fight.

Maybe lots of us just share a soul.

So there's no judgement, because there's no point.

It was just this stupid idea.

But it was in my head like a block or something.

Curly-haired Patricia was there with me at the funeral.

I'd been getting on the bus a lot recently, spending a lot of time down there in Parliament Street.

And later on we were in the pub.

And I was staring down at the tiles on the floor.

Because I knew that she was a fighter, and I had the other soul.

And it was more than just a sneaky suspicion that if she was going to fight for me, that I was going to go with the flow.

14

DERMOT

Understandably, I felt like a man who'd been shot up into the air and all the lads with the nets had fucked off.

And I was coming down to Earth.

Down to Dublin.

Down the back of the plane in economy.

I was like a zombie.

Standing there outside the airport waiting on a taxi.

And when I got one your man is very much on for a big chat.

Where had I been? How was it? What did I do for a living myself?

Holy fuck. I was like one of those figures you see in the religious paintings where God is pointing for them all to go to Hell. And they're all looking up at him, very much feeling the reality of their situation.

I lugged my suitcase into the hall and I could see Mary and Colm out the back garden.

They'd pulled the kitchen table out on the grass so they could have their lunch in the sun.

I took a chair and went out and joined them.

We had ham and boiled eggs and brown bread and tea and a jug of Miwadi orange.

Colm started kicking a ball around but I didn't have the energy.

I just sat there and told Mary the job was gone.

That it was a mistake.

She laughed at me in a way I understood.

That it was inevitable that things like that should happen to me. That I was someone to whom things happened.

Colm came over for a drink of orange and absent-mindedly his arm was on the back of my chair and I could hear him slurping his drink and he absent-mindedly ran one of his fingers over the stubble on my cheek.

And that he felt entitled to do that . . .

I remembered the day he was born.

The first time I held him in my arms.

I thought I'd feel responsible.

But I didn't really feel anything.

I remember when he learned to read.

The relief I felt because I didn't have to sit beside his bed any more.

I turned around but he was gone.

And Mary just said to me:

'When I met you, do you know why I chose you?

Because I felt sorry for you.

You looked so woebegone that none of the girls would dance with you.

You looked so scared there with all the other boys.

And remember. I was no mean looker in them days, Dermot, I had long legs and I had big boobs and a big blondy dye job in my hair.

And all the boys you were standing there with, they couldn't believe me walking past them and asking you to dance.

Sure you couldn't believe it yourself!

'What?' You said to me.

You fucking eejit.

What!

I nearly had to drag you to your feet.

You were shaking there on the dancefloor.

You were shaking in my arms.

When I planted a kiss on you, you didn't know what to do.

You got the hang of it.

But it took you a minute.

You held on to me like you were afraid you were going to wake up and I'd be gone.

I'd been with loads of fellas before you.

But they were all obvious for me.

They all had a smart mouth because their mammies had turned them into mickey dazzlers telling them the sun, moon and stars shone out of their heads.

But I shut them up.

Because I wasn't a girl who was afraid to put her hand down a boy's underpants.

I could make a boy do anything I wanted.

But I chose you, Dermot, because you were alone in the world.

And I knew you probably would be for the rest of your life and I decided that I was going to be your friend.

And I know you don't think much of me anymore.

And I don't care you take me for granted and I know I embarrass you because I never lost all this weight after Colm.

But I chose you Dermot.

I took you because I knew you'd always need someone to look after you. And I always will,' she said.

And it was like I was looking at the three of us there in the garden from high above.

I could see Colm banging an orange football around down there against the concrete walls.

And I could see me and Mary sitting there at the table.

Her hand was on the back of my head.

And I was like a hunched figure.

My face falling slowly into her lap.

15

JOE

When you live in close proximity to people in a home like me, and you're fairly private, you don't let on if you've got news.

Especially if it's of a highly personal nature.

So to look at me walking around with this photo in my pocket you wouldn't know a thing.

But Sister Pat clocked me a few times, that I was miles away.

And I had to get out of her gaze.

Jackie Fennel thought it was bloody Christmas when I suggested we go and get a bottle of stout at one o'clock in the afternoon.

And then Mary Larkin got in on the act.

And of course it was a big event now and everyone was clucking around that the three of us were turning into alcoholics.

But what can you do?

So there we were hobbling round to Tighe's in the sunshine.

Jackie was the most agile.

He could still do two things at once.

He was counting out his change, not needing to look where he was going.

Mary Larkin was going on about what a beautiful day it was but that didn't stop her ducking into Tighe's where it was all suitably dark and empty, and drinking five bottles of Harp.

She was buckled by half two.

We had the place to ourselves.

Jackie kept fiddling with the telly, looking for the racing, until the barman gave in and let him have the remote control.

And although I was joining in the general conversation, I was secretly in a world of my own.

Thinking about Marion Ross and why she'd had this picture sent to me.

I'd had a look in Jackie's backlog of *Independents* and I was right.

She'd passed away a few weeks before.

And I was thinking that she was right in a way.

If I wanted a picture of her, why shouldn't I have it?

And if you can be friends, what are you afraid of?

Except of course what had happened was that I'd fallen in love with someone I didn't know and that was all there was about it.

And I never knew her, but when it hits you, it just does.

And maybe if I'd gotten to know her I mightn't even have liked her, but there you are. I know it exists.

But, I made a decision and your life runs its course.

Maybe I could've battled my way around to us ending up together.

But what can I say?

It just wasn't in me.

I'm just not made like that.

And a few bottles of stout and two or three balls of malt later we made our way back around to the home.

Mary Larkin was singing 'You Are My Sunshine, My Only Sunshine', but she shut up when Sister Pat hoved into view.

Jackie Fennel was doing a little dance and rubbing his hands together.

'We're home from the fields!' he says to Sister Pat.

And we sat down and had our dinner.

And of course we were the talk of the bloody town.

'Whose birthday was it?' and all this.

Poor Mary had to hit the sack around seven o'clock.

But Jackie was taking them all on.

He was in great form, slagging them all off.

But then, suddenly, he was fading fast.

And Sister Pat put him to bed.

And I sat there on my own in the dining room.

They didn't think anyone was in there so the lights were off.

But Sister Pat came and found me and we went down to her room and had a cup of tea.

And although she was furious I hadn't told her what I'd gotten in the post, the problem was that she liked me too much to give me a hard time.

So we just chatted about this and that and she told me all about where she'd grown up in Roscommon.

And soon enough it was time for bed.

And when I had my pyjamas on I went over to the table and took these rosary beads out that used to belong to Liz that she'd gotten in Lourdes.

And I had them sort of wrapped around my fingers.

And naturally I took Marion's photograph out of my jacket and I looked at it for a little while.

This little girl staring up out at me.

A big smile on her.

Very happy.

Someone I didn't know.

And I was slightly too knackered to finish the last couple of pages of this cowboy book I was reading.

So I just lay back with Marion's picture in one hand and Liz's
   rosary beads in the other.

Thinking about regret and worry.

And when you get to my age, you give up on them because
   they don't help anything.

And you generally get tired of regret.

And you're usually just whacked out from worrying.

So I brought these two things together on my chest.

The picture and the beads.

On my heart if you like.

And I did what any Christian would do.

I turned out the light and I went to sleep.

COME ON OVER

Come On Over was first performed at the Gate Theatre, Dublin, on 27 September 2001. The cast was as follows:

MATTHEW   Jim Norton

MARGARET   Dearbhla Molloy

Director   Conor McPherson
Designer   Eileen Diss
Lighting Designer   Mick Hughes

Characters

MATTHEW

MARGARET

There are two chairs onstage.

MATTHEW *and* MARGARET *enter together from the same side.*

They both wear plain clothes and hoods.

The hoods should look like mass-produced sacking and have neat holes for the eyes and mouth.

Margaret might wear a simple silver-chain necklace.

They sit and regard the audience.

MATTHEW.

There were tomato plants spiralling up these sticks there in the window ledge.

The sunlight was coming in through all the leaves.

Me and Margaret were looking at them and counting the tomatoes.

I was shocked at how she'd aged.

We'd hardly said a thing since I came in. In off the main street and into her narrow hallway and up the stairs into the spare room.

Her daughter had planted these tomatoes before she'd left to go on her travels.

Margaret watered them and I put my suitcase down and sat on the bed.

Outside, the little town was dead.

So many shopfronts boarded up.

The silence was overwhelming.

The house where I grew up was gone.

I'd stepped off the bus into my past.

Into the shocking reality of myself and everything I'd been through.

Margaret turned away from the plants towards me and took my hand for a moment before she left and I heard her go downstairs.

I'd spent the last two months recovering from an experience I'd had in Africa.

I'd slept and dreamed and prayed in a seminary in Belgium until Father Sebarus came to see me.

He was as sympathetic as always but also businesslike because he was my boss.

He held an A4 envelope on his lap while he sat there gravely talking to me.

I didn't feel any terror any more but even though I was medicated I sensed that the envelope would change me even further than I'd already gone.

Maybe even back to what I had been.

MARGARET.

I was watering Nuala's tomatoes.

Matthew. Father Matthew sat behind me on the bed.

I stood looking down at them much longer than I needed to because I was starting to cry.

He seemed so old.

This boy I once knew.

And the tomatoes were reminding me, do you see, of a day thirty-odd years ago when we'd taken a walk in the rose gardens in the park. It was October and it was the last of the roses.

He was always huddled in his big coat and I'd always have my hand in his pocket. Holding his hand.

And I loved him so much.

I always remember that day, in the rose gardens.

With the roses dying. And him miles away.

And me wanting to tell him that I'd worn a skirt instead of trousers because I wanted him to touch me.

But I knew I'd already lost him.

He was lost.

MATTHEW.

Father Sebarus wanted me to look into this one for a few reasons. Well namely the main one was because it had happened in the town I was born in.

He opened the envelope and in it were photographs of a little girl maybe thirteen or fourteen.

She was asleep and someone had placed blue flowers all around her. She was a corpse.

She'd been found in the graveyard at St Monica's, the parish I'd grown up in.

They'd sold some land there and when they were moving some coffins, hers had burst open.

And everyone nearly died.

Because she was perfectly preserved.

She'd been buried four hundred years ago.

MARGARET.

Matthew was a Jesuit. He was a scientist.

He'd been all over the world looking into what I suppose people thought were miracles.

He was a very rational sort of person.

And although I hadn't seen him for many years I could tell from his letters that he was reluctant to give his imprimatur that he had ever come across anything that was really a miracle. I suppose he saw a rational cause for everything.

And he'd always been like that.

I was shocked naturally when he said he thought he had a vocation all those years ago.

But there had always been a kindness in him. And I loved him for it.

And he was so courageous taking such a huge step.

I respected him, naturally, and I supported him.

But I don't think I need to tell you that it broke my heart.

MATTHEW.

I had a restless night.

It was deathly quiet.

But more than that it was a quiet I'd grown up with, and at about three or half three in the morning I went into the bathroom and took some toilet roll.

And I took it back into my room and I cried my fucking eyes out, 'til I thought I couldn't breathe.

I thought then that I heard Margaret stirring so I put the light out and I waited until it started to get bright and I began to feel slightly better.

Almost dreading and wanting to get to work.

A car was picking me up at eight.

And it's not good for a man to lie there all night terrified.

It's not right.

MARGARET.

I had his breakfast ready at seven.

He came down all neat and shaven.

But he couldn't really eat.

When I'd ran the B&B anyone that passed through, the salesmen'd usually go to town on the brekkie, so I was, it was a bit of a habit. I was piling toast and eggs and the best of rashers and sausages in front of him. But he just drank some tea.

Apologising to me. Always apologising. But all he did was smoke Silk Cut reds and drink his tea.

His leg was shaking under the table.

So I ignored him and left him to his smoke and his tea and I sat in the drawing room with that old clock ticking 'til I heard his car arrive and the mad scratch of his chair on the kitchen floor like God Himself had come to save him.

MATTHEW.

They'd left the body in the little church.

You could see all our breaths.

The chap from UCD's phone kept going off. He was saying something about organic substances buried below the permafrost. A woman from Trinity supervised students taking soil samples. But I felt detached.

Because something else was happening.

This child. She just looked asleep.

Her fair hair and the flowers around her.

The only clue was her sunken eyes.

And my hands shook outside while Father Sebarus gave me a light. And it wasn't just the shock of something so weird and out of the ordinary.

It was . . . I knew I'd just laid eyes on the most beautiful thing I'd ever seen.

And so much of me was longing not to be inspired because . . . well, because I'd lost my faith a long time ago. And something in me was begging to be free.

And Father Sebarus was looking at me so intently that I had to turn away and walk through the gravestones because if I didn't I was going to turn and smash his face in.

MARGARET.

My husband, Patrick, died from leukemia in hospital in Galway. I was with him when he died.

He was hardly there any more.

He was a good man. Big fingers like potatoes. A big man. But in the end he was just skin and bone.

I sort of wanted to get into the bed there with him at the end. Sort of to remind myself what it was like to share a bed with someone. Under the covers. A man and a woman. What brings them together, you know? I wanted to see what it was like again. I wanted everyone to go. I was holding his hand when he went.

Nuala finished in UCG and went off on her travels.

I looked after Patrick's father. We looked after each other. He wasn't a bother.

Always asking me why I'd get so fret up about things.

'Sit down there now and have a cup of tea,' he'd say.

He'd peel an orange the way he used to when Nuala was a toddler, giving her bits while she pootered around, coming over, getting orange all over his lap.

He'd lean on his stick and look out the window in the kitchen.

He'd trace his finger round the edge of the ashtray.

And I'd write to Father Matthew, knowing how much he needed kind words, out there somewhere in South America or somewhere, knowing how much he needed, well, the same as what I felt Nuala needed when she rang from Boston or San Fransisco. And how much she missed her dad.

And her granddad.

And it was always around these times that I took down all the net curtains to wash them. I don't know why. Like a stupid candle in the bloody window.

MATTHEW.

I went back on my own that night.

A little sacristan called Jerry opened the chapel for me. I can't forget the stars.

They were above us and down all across the graveyard.

He turned on the lights and left me there to pray.

But it wasn't really prayer.

I was just thinking about the corpse.

I . . . loved her.

It was like she'd travelled this long distance. All this way, so I could see her.

You see, I was so alone. And I needed to see her again.

But they'd packed her in a thermal case and taken her to Dublin.

I'm a racist.

Blacks and whites age differently.

To me they do.

MARGARET.

I have no problem saying this.

I had one of Matthew's V-neck sweaters up to my face.

When I sucked in I was breathing him in through my nose.

The tops of my legs were leaning against his bed.

I folded it for him and lay it with his few clothes.

Taking in his washing I'd looked up and never seen so many stars.

I went into the kitchen, turned off the light in the yard, and came back out in the dark.

I'd got into this habit. Of doing whatever I felt like.

Ha ha. There was a dance the Pioneers had in Jamestown every month.

I always went and danced with my seventy-year-old bachelor who wasn't a pioneer at all. They actually always had drink there for him!

I put my nose on his shoulder and took in all the turf and cigarettes.

Slow waltz. Lovely.

Whatever I felt like.

But. Em. Smelling jumpers in my own house.

MATTHEW (*to* MARGARET). I was lost.

MARGARET (*to* MATTHEW). Stop.

Keep going, I'm sorry.

MATTHEW (*to audience*). Something dreadful happened to me.

MARGARET (*to* MATTHEW). Matthew . . .

MATTHEW (*to* MARGARET). You don't understand.

MARGARET (*to* MATTHEW). I . . . didn't mean to interrupt you. I'm sorry. I didn't think I was going to.

MATTHEW (*to audience*).

When I was in Africa, I . . .

I went to the home of an Englishman to . . . to talk with him. Because he'd been . . . seeing a girl. A young girl. A child.

I suspected that he was . . . abusing her.

She was eleven. Her name was Patience.

I'd first seen her under a tree in the shade where she was helping a nurse inoculating babies and children from the school.

She was a bright girl.

She seemed older.

She looked like a woman. I mean a small grown woman.

It was the nurse who told me. Her suspicion about Patience and this English gentleman.

And you see, my faith was very strong then.

I mean I knew why we were here.

We were here to love God.

God was the law. God was the word.

(*To* MARGARET.) We don't even have time for this!

MARGARET (*to* MATTHEW). Well. Go on. Because I have things to say.

MATTHEW *regards her and regards the audience. He reaches into his pocket and takes out a box of tablets. He drops them. He picks them up and drops them again a few times during the following.*

MATTHEW.

When I drop these tablets. They fall to the ground.

I know that when I let them go, they'll never float up into the air or stay hanging where I release them.

They'll always fall to the ground.

Always. And I know why.

I'd spent thirty years, more, just reflecting.

And the idea I had, the idea I had which became the truth for me, was that the tablets or anything I let go of will fall to the ground because something wants them to.

Something is willing the way things are.

The way everything is.

And that will is God.

This was quite plain to me. It was just that simple.

I don't claim that I've always been in my right mind but years and years in the library . . .

Years and years of order . . .

I don't want to say that it was just seductive.

Because I wasn't weak.

But I had drawn my own conclusions. And I believed in what I believed in. I had beliefs.

And I went to the home of this Englishman and I confronted him.

And I was almost manic in my fervour because I knew what I was talking about.

He went pale, staring at his carpet and his pool.

But ultimately I pitied him and I shook his hand and I left.

But going down the dirt road, I began to see waves in front of my eyes.

It was the beginning of a migraine.

I could only see anything on the right-hand side of my vision.

And I saw Patience on the road coming towards me, going up to the Englishman's house.

I wanted to stop her and talk to her. We spoke often and we were very close.

But my headache was becoming crippling and I just smiled and walked past her. And she stopped and watched me march by.

All I cared about was getting into a dark room and putting a cold cloth on my head.

So I went to bed and my housekeeper brought me some tea and I slept.

But something woke me.

It was dark. It was dusk. Someone was in the room.

I was groggy and I turned on the lamp.

Patience had let herself in. She had a key.

I . . . pulled back the covers, telling myself again for the tenth time that this'd be the last time.

I was waiting for her to get in.

And she shoved a big knife into my face.

She shoved it in and out four times.

I lost this eye and half my nose and the knife ended up embedded in between my teeth, in my gum here.

She couldn't get it out again, which is what saved me.

MARGARET.

He was due to go up to Dublin in the morning.

And we sat eating our dinner.

Pork chops.

And I just came out with it.

I asked him to stay.

I said stay here.

Do you remember, I said, do you remember it was one St Brigid's Day and all the Holy Faith girls had the day off. I had a skirt on. We went for a walk in the rose gardens. It was October, all the roses were dying.

You broke my heart.

MATTHEW.

That can't be right, I said.

St Brigid's Day isn't in October. It's in the Spring.

MARGARET.

Whatever. I heard him toss and turn until about one or half one. He went to the toilet five or six times.

I was dropping off when I felt his weight on the bed.

He was sitting there and I put my hand out and I rubbed his shoulders for a while.

And he lay down with his back to me and I kept rubbing him 'til he calmed down and his breathing became a bit slower. Then I put my arm around his tummy.

She takes off her hood.

And I could feel his . . . He was hard. He was gently pressing it against the inside of my arm here.

MATTHEW (*to* MARGARET). Put it back on.

MARGARET. And I felt the knot where he'd tied the top of his pyjama bottoms. I was picking at it.

MATTHEW. I'm not denying any of this but I think you should put it back on.

MARGARET. I gripped him as hard as I could. It was my left hand and I'm right-handed. And while he . . . pushed himself back and forth these were the thoughts I had:

MATTHEW. Please put it back on.

MARGARET. His was the first erect penis I'd touched when I was a girl. And Patrick's was the next and here I was holding it again and I was wondering where it had been.

MATTHEW. Margaret . . .

MARGARET. And I was thinking about Nuala and how many she'd felt.

MATTHEW. Margaret . . .

MARGARET. She's in New York. I don't care what you say about how cheap it is to fly anywhere. She's thousands of miles away and I want to see her. I want her here.

MATTHEW. Margaret, put your hood on.

MARGARET (*to* MATTHEW). You're no good.

I'd take you in. I don't care about your face.

MATTHEW. Don't do this to yourself.

MARGARET. You coward.

She regards him. She finally puts the hood back on.

MATTHEW.

In the morning, before I left, there was a call.

The body had started to rot.

It was decomposing in Dublin.

Pause.

When Patience attacked me I was a sinner.

MARGARET. You coward.

MATTHEW. But the greatest sin was to feel abandoned.

And not to trust in God's love.

MARGARET. You coward.

MATTHEW. Not to trust in God.

MARGARET. Love me.

MATTHEW.

Not trusting God was my greatest sin.

But he sent me this little girl.

Preserved for hundreds of years. To forgive me.

MARGARET. No . . .

MATTHEW.

It was his way of forgiving me.

And I knew I had to hurry.

Because I was going to say I'd finally seen a miracle.

And I knew I'd probably have a fight on my hands.

So I got moving.

MARGARET *gets up and goes to* MATTHEW.

She embraces him.

He leans his head into her.

End.

AFTERWORD
an interview with Carol Vander

Carol Vander *Could we begin by asking you how you write – do you write every day?*

Conor McPherson Well, no . . . I say that and then I think, actually I do write quite a lot. I'm probably confused because for me, writing is just something I do, sort of on the way to something else. Like, when I am writing a play, I am already thinking about the actual show, rather than looking at it as a piece of writing . . .

So the idea is already strongly formed?

Well, yes and no. It is like a weird memory of something, or a murky dream you are trying to piece back together when you wake up. I suppose it all comes from the unconscious. But at the same time I am consciously trying to shape it into something which makes sense and has an internal logic.

But you know what you are trying to achieve when you sit down to write – you always know where the story is going . . .

Oh yeah! I could never sit down to a blank piece of paper and not have a clue where I am going. That, to me, is a nightmare! The great thing about the writing process is that it sort of slows your thought down, so day by day, ideas are coming organically and the good ones make sense and the bad ones are, hopefully, pretty obvious. So they're coming in, and I'm filing them away in my brain for the next day while I am writing up ideas which maybe are weeks or months or years old.

You have said before that if writers are like athletes, you are a sprinter as opposed to a long-distance runner.

Yes. The show is the finish line and that's where I want to be. Not at the show, but in rehearsals.

So do you go through many changes, do you work with a dramaturge in a particular theatre?

No, never. I don't go there. I write the thing and then I try to put it on as it is. Naturally it'll change in rehearsals. Actors will often start doing it and things become apparent immediately. And what usually becomes apparent to me is what we don't need. Whole speeches or whatever. But you know what? You can usually spot that when you are writing it anyway, and seeing the actors performing it will just confirm your suspicions. Funnily, this is a reason why I prefer directing my own stuff. You can just cut a whole page out there and then and move on. But if you are working with a director, he or she is obviously more nervous about that, and suddenly you find you are fighting someone who wants to keep something in. They just want to be sure that everything is happening in a way that makes sense, but I need to go by my gut and not have to discuss everything too much.

But don't you have to show your script to the artistic director of a theatre or a producer to get it produced?

Oh yeah, of course you do, but if someone were to say to me, 'This needs to be changed' or 'We need another character', or something, I'm more likely to try and go somewhere else where they understand it as it is, rather than change it.

Is this a recent development or were you always like that?

I was always like that!

You used to run your own theatre company, didn't you?

Well, 'run' and 'theatre company' are probably going a bit far! When we left college, there was me and Peter McDonald, Kevin Hely, Colin O'Connor, a whole group of people, Jason Byrne – the director, not the comedian, and we were just these people who had got turned on to the theatre while we were students in UCD. We lived down in the bowels of the building in the basement where the drama society was, putting on plays, sitting in the bar, philosophising and plotting and dreaming, you know, and then when we left the university we wanted to continue so, you know, we had to find somewhere to put plays on . . .

You were all working together?

Yeah . . . we were . . . we had all developed an understanding of each other and we knew what we were good at. Me and Collie, Colin O'Connor, were the ones who always wrote the plays. Pete McDonald and Kevin Hely were the actors, you know . . .

So your plays were designed for that group . . .

Yeah, I suppose . . . I mean the only place we could afford to put plays on was the International Bar on Wicklow Street. I wrote this little play called *Radio Play*, which was a bunch of strange little sketches really, all set in and around a late night radio talk show, and we were all in it, me and Kevin . . .

You were acting in it?

Sure! Everybody did everything at that time. And that little show . . . we did it for two weeks, every day at lunchtime. And we gave everybody free sandwiches. We called ourselves The Fly By Night Theatre Company, and that show was a hit. It was full every day. We had managed to get some free ads on the radio through going around trying to get sponsorship – sell ad space in the programme – and a new radio station did a deal with us and advertised our show for nothing. I say it was full – the capacity was forty people – but there were forty people there every day – at lunchtime! One o'clock! And you have to remember we didn't have a clue what we were doing . . . This was our first step out in the big bad world as artists and it worked, so . . .

So you kept going?

Yeah, well, we tried . . . but it was tough. I wrote another one, and Collie wrote one and we booked the International Bar for a month to do these lunchtime plays. You know, to get the money to pay for it, we'd put on ties and jackets and go around local businesses in the area trying to get people to buy ads . . . it was really fly by night!

But good training I'd say . . .

Well, good training . . . I don't know, but it certainly gave any of us involved with it a feeling of independence. It showed me that you can do all this stuff yourself. I was never one for writing something and sending it somewhere to some genius in some theatre somewhere and waiting around with my fingers crossed. I still kind of have that hands-on thing. I'll go and bang the door somewhere myself to get something going, it doesn't bother me.

So what happened to the theatre company?

Well like I say, it was tough and we all needed to make a living . . .

How old were you?

We were like, twenty-one or twenty-two . . .

Young!

Yeah, young, very young. We knew nothing. And we all had to get jobs. I think I was always convinced I was going to start making money as a playwright and so I only ever had a little part-time job on the go or whatever – no career. But others in the group began to get a little restless and there was nothing happening in Ireland at that time. It was before the whole Celtic Tiger thing, so people started to go abroad looking for work or getting a job if they could so . . . you know . . . it dwindled down a lot. The make-or-break thing for me was when me and Kevin Hely decided to go for it and rent the City Arts Centre for two weeks and do my play, *The Light of Jesus* as it was called then. It's called *The Good Thief* now.

We raised a grand each, or something. It was a one-man show, and Kevin performed it. And, well, no one came, but it really changed things for me in a few ways. We lost all our money, and disgracefully we fell out during the run! It was horrible! Poor Kevin was performing the play every night and we weren't speaking to each other.

Oh no . . .

I know! It was horrible . . . but one night, nobody at all showed up and I had to go and tell Kevin that the show was cancelled, and we just started laughing and everything was alright after that! But a few critics saw it and we got some cracking reviews. But by the time they came out, the show was gone. But there was some interest in it at least then.

Because of the reviews?

Yeah, sort of . . . a bunch of people started saying, 'This can't just disappear . . . ' So like, there was a journalist called Mic Moroney who saw it and organised for us to have like a one-off performance of it at the Project Arts Centre. And people who missed it, or felt they should have seen it or whatever, came. And my cousin, Garret Keogh, who's an actor, came and asked if he could perform it. He was well known because he was the baddie in an Irish soap opera called *Fair City*. It's a very popular show. So we went on the road with it, and people came, because they knew him, and then it won an award, the Stewart Parker award, so . . .

So you were finally . . .

Well, I don't know if I was 'finally' anything! But it gave me a little bit more confidence in what I was doing.

Your next play This Lime Tree Bower, *that really changed things for you, didn't it?*

Yeah, that was the one. People will always associate me with the success of *The Weir*, but *Lime Tree* was where I felt I really hit something. Where it really connected with the audience. That was huge play for me.

Why do you think that was?

It was just . . . ballsier . . . is that a word?

I think so!

Yeah, it . . . had a good . . . it was just more, I don't know, confidence, a bit of a swing to it. Good show too . . .

You directed it, right?

Yeah, well by this time Fly By Night wasn't happening really. People had gone away or packed in the theatre stuff to earn a living, you know, so I was a little bit stranded. But I thought, you know, for the first time, 'Hey why am I breaking my arse trying to put these things on myself all the time?' Why don't

I send it to some theatres and see if they'll do it, you know, the way it's supposed to! So I sent it around a few places, but it didn't . . . connect or . . .

Where did you send it?

Well, the usual suspects in Dublin, the Abbey, the Gate, the Project, RTE. But no one wanted it. Although I did get a meeting at the Abbey, which was a big deal for me.

But they didn't produce it.

No. They wanted me to write another character in it.

Who?

Someone 'good' is what they wanted. So we'd know that the other characters were 'bad' I suppose. But I felt that the ambiguity of it was kind of the point of the whole thing so . . .

You didn't meet anyone else?

Em . . . no . . . I don't think so. I was lucky to know a guy called Philip Gray who was running the Crypt Arts Centre in Dublin Castle. He was a funny guy who I always got on with, and he helped me to put it on there for the first Fringe Festival, and it was great. It was packed every night. Terrific reviews. And that's what my agent, Nick Marston, saw first and he took me on. I met him in the pub across the road. I was put onto him by Paddy Breathnach and Rob Walpole who I was writing *I Went Down* for at the time. And within about ten months we were off to London to do it at the Bush.

Which changed things enormously.

Well, yeah! It was great I was getting paid! But I was also writing a movie by then, which was a big hit at that time, so a whole lot of things took off. *Lime Tree* bagged a whole load of awards in London. I became the Bush's writer in residence. It was amazing! I was getting published. It was fantastic. I couldn't believe it.

And it started your relationship with audiences in London.

Yes! Well they became the people who accepted my work, and wanted it! So it was a great feeling. It was a real fresh start. It was like I had somehow got to a place where I couldn't believe it. I was going to the airport, getting on a plane, going to London. And this was my job! I mean, there's a self-consciousness which creeps in, you know, 'Who am I?', 'What's going on?' Slightly weird.

What do you mean?

I don't know. It's like 80% of doing anything creative is the guts to do it, I think. The self-doubt that accompanies anything creative is pretty horrible. Fairly existential! If you're young and you are just going for it, okay, there's a mindless energy there which will keep it going. But when you get to that place where, you know, the *Guardian* and the *Times* and the *Independent* and the *Financial Times* and the *Observer* are all writing articles about what a great writer you are, and I was like, what, 25? It's weird because you realise, 'These are the bastions of all this fairly literary culture and they rate me pretty highly . . . ' but at the same time you're like, 'Hold on. I thought that if I ever got to this point I'd *know* something!' But I didn't know anything – of course I didn't!

But know what?

I don't know. Something about life?

Did you feel like a phoney?

No, not like I was fooling anyone, because I could see that audiences were definitely getting a bang for their buck. But just that personally, I don't think I understood what was sustaining me as a writer. But just a huge amount of energy and drive, and I had no idea where it was coming from.

So you were a hot young playwright on the London scene. What happened next?

Well, the Bush wanted another play. And the Royal Court were asking me to write a play. I was writing *St Nicholas* anyway, and I'd had the idea for *The Weir* already, so I was kind of stuck into those. And they were both written around the same time.

In St Nicholas *a distasteful theatre critic starts working for vampires . . . where did that come from?*

Deep!! I don't know. Fear . . . all that stuff about recognition . . .
would it last . . . anger . . . all that. I'd met a bunch of theatre
critics by this stage and I recognised something in them. Their
interest in people and drama is huge, but somehow made
'safe' by watching plays all the time. Honest writing is raw. It
hurts the writer in ways. It has too. But it's a necessity. Otherwise you go crazy. And to have a character like that who *can't
write* but wants to, and writes reviews of other writers. That
just seemed like black gold for me. And I just dove in there.
That play has a good dark power in it. And it's also quite real
for me . . .

But isn't it the most fantasy-like play you've written?

Yes! But what's real and what's fantasy? I mean he follows an
actress to London and makes a fool of himself and starts to work
for, and is saved in a way by, dark forces closer to the imagination than anything. It was my story in many ways. That's
what was real about it for me. But at the time I wouldn't have
seen it like that. I just approached it in a bullish way. I was just
like a kamikaze. I wanted to push it, to burn it up. Destroy it
maybe. Weird.

Was it a shift of gear working with a star, Brian Cox?

It was great working with him. What work? I just had to be
there with him, that's all. He has the mysterious power that
good actors have. He just stands in front of people and they
watch him. They have to. He is compelling. So to have that in
your arsenal was just amazing. And we got on great. I loved
him. He looked out for me too. Always gave me a place to stay
when I went to London. It really took the sting out of going to
that big city alone.

*Some critics started to complain about all these monologues.
Did you write* The Weir *in response to that?*

No way! I'd love to be able to tailor my writing to change it
around to suit everybody – who wouldn't? It shows how little
critics understand about writing when they expect someone to
just turn tack on their say so. Writers write what they write
because they *have* to. Otherwise they can't live. It's not that
kind of thing you can control. Anyway, why should I have to

please them, and write like some other writer? There are lots of
writers doing different things. Why should I write something
that someone else is doing or has already done? It's such a
stupid, lazy complaint, in my opinion.

*But a stick used to beat many playwrights, the whole
monologue thing.*

Sure. And look, I understand that. You really sweep away so
many of the pleasurable things about theatre when you chop it
down to one voice. But people were going for it. They liked it.
They wanted it. Full houses. So I was lucky, it didn't matter
what those kinds of critics said. And *St Nicholas* was my first
play to hit New York, and it was a huge hit there. That's the
play they knew me for – they had no problem with it.

Do you think you are defensive when it comes to reviews?

Yes! Defensive is an understatement! I think I feel so close to
what I do. I really feel it so painfully if my work is misunder-
stood or dismissed. I shouldn't read reviews. But I'll still
complain that I have yet to learn anything from a success or
a good review so . . . I'm basically angry and confused!

Before we talk about The Weir, *let's just finish up the
monologue thing. You directed Eugene O'Brien's first play,*
Eden, *a huge success at the Abbey a few years ago, was it the
monologues that attracted you?*

Well, just the writing. And I suppose the monologues didn't
intimidate me or get in the way of my enjoyment of it. I don't
know if that was his first play. He had done a few things I
think, but they were on the way to *Eden*, as it were, some of
the characters in *Eden* were already there. I didn't know him.
I was just sent the script. I identified with it and I directed it.
It was the period in my life where I was drinking heavily. I was
drinking before rehearsals in the fucking morning, Carol! The
relationship I was in was in total tatters. And I poured that
energy into the show. I didn't give a fuck. Any note of false-
ness, or something I didn't relate to, that the actors were doing,
I was on them like a hot snot.

*What did they think about working with you when you were
drinking?*

I don't know, it was crazy . . . it was crazy. But they knew
I understood the play. They could see I was in an enormous
amount of pain, pissed, crazy, but they wanted me to continue;
Eugene and Catherine Walsh and Don Wicherley. It was mad!
I said 'I can't do this!' But they didn't want to let go of what
we had and I didn't really want to stop, because I knew the
play was so great and the actors were giving it 110% – so we
kept going. Eugene really hit something deep in the Irish
people with that play. They came in their droves to see it. It
was too successful in many ways because I had to keep coming
back to re-direct it for more runs. It transferred from the little
Peacock stage up to the Abbey main stage, and it sold out!
That never happens! It was a fantastic beginning to Eugene's
career as a playwright and great performances from Don and
Catherine. I was happy to be a part of it, but like I say, a crazy,
crazy time. That play went on for years, and finally ended up
in the West End of all places!

*We will probably come back to that 'craziness' but if I can just
ask you . . . You are probably sick of talking about* The Weir,
*but can you tell me a bit about what it was like when that all
happened?*

Well, it was weird for me because when I wrote it for the
Royal Court, it was going to be for Ian Rickson to direct. So
that was strange, working with a director. But, God, I was so
lucky. He really saw stuff in the play that he understood and
related to. He was so careful with it. He was so detailed. He
involved me all the way, casting, I was at all the auditions. I
was at the first week of rehearsal and then left them to it for a
few weeks and came back in the last week.

The most intriguing part for me, for all of us, was the great set
by Rae Smith. The audience were sitting *in the bar* on all these
little higgledy-piggledy different kinds of chairs and benches.
You were right in on top of the action. It was great. And it
had like a little four-week run. But the demand for tickets was
phenomenal, so they extended it for a few weeks. And then
a few more. And then they had to move it to a bigger theatre.
And suddenly they were telling me things like, 'This is the
fastest-selling show in the history of the Royal Court.' It was
unbelievable. I had these cheques coming in week after week,

just for sitting on my arse at home in Dublin. I was involved in
my film stuff at the time so I wasn't as much on hand, so as it
went through recasts and all that, I left it to Ian, who, God love
him, was living with that play for a few years.

*But you went to see it in New York. I first met you there around
that time.*

Yeah. When we finished filming *Saltwater* I went over to see it
on Broadway. I hadn't been able to go to the early part of the
run. My mum had gone for the opening night! Her sister flew
in from California. They had a blast. She was doing interviews
with the press and everything. It was wild! She rang me at
like four in the morning and read the *New York Times* review
down the phone from the restaurant where the party was. And
it was a great review so they were all going mad, and I said,
'What about the other reviews?' And I could hear the restaurant
manager there in the background shouting, 'They don't matter!'
So all that was going on. Weird.

*You keep saying everything is weird! Weren't you wildly
happy?*

No. I was far from it. Success in your work teaches you fuck
all, except that you're good at your job. So what? It's true what
they say. You can have money and fame and riches, but if you're
not happy inside . . . you're not happy.

Why weren't you happy?

Oh it's all too horrible and boring to go into here. But I found
living my life and being alive so fucking scary and painful that
I had to drink to kill the fear. But that cycle you get stuck in is
a nightmare. And it'll kill you. And it almost killed me.

We met again in New York when you came to direct Dublin
Carol *at the Atlantic in 2003. You seemed like a man on a
mission. Why was it so important to you to come and direct it?*

Well, it was the play I wrote in the aftermath of the success of
The Weir. It's a hugely personal play. I was really excavating
the darkness and the whole alcohol thing. Ian directed the first
production with Brian Cox and Bronagh Gallagher and
Andrew Scott, a dream cast. But I felt removed from the whole

event. They are great actors and Ian gave it everything, but it was too painful for me to relate to at that time. It was like staring into a nightmare of all my fears. So a few years later, when I got sober, it was really important for me to revisit it and put it to rest by engaging in it and directing it.

It was also a wonderful production in New York. Jim Norton was astonishing. You must have been delighted when he won the Obie award for Best Actor.

Oh, I was thrilled for him! It was a tough rehearsal. I really went at it. I had to. And Kerry O'Malley and Keith Nobbs, the two American actors were fantastic. They worked so fucking hard on the accent. It was a great thing to do. I love working with Jim. He's the real thing. And a real gentleman.

And you cast him in Port Authority *too.*

I sure did. That was all around the same time as *Eden* and just before I collapsed. Mad. I was so lucky to have those actors, Jim, Stephen Brennan, Eanna MacLiam. No messing around. I was gone fucking nuts by that stage.

But you got the reviews of your life for that one. Dare I say it, some people may have even liked it more than The Weir.

Unbelievable. That show was like a rocket going off. Really simple, but something strong was making the whole place vibrate. The whole live experience. It was like the guy who wrote *Lime Tree Bower* coming back with another one, with a few more years experience under his belt – which it was!

And you were back to monologues . . .

Yeah. I was trying to write about my feelings. About love, really. And I just needed the freedom of the monologues to go there. I needed the weaponry. But I've just been so lucky to have the opportunity to show my work to people, and then if you hit some miraculous thing – *they get it*!! But I still have to say that I find the idea of watching my own work very painful.

Which brings us to Come On Over . . .

Yeah. Like all my little lame children, but I love that little play.

But you say you find your work painful?

It's complex. Like love. You know? That play is like a little kid who's hidden under the bed after a tantrum and everything is calmed down and you go to get the kid and they roar at you from under the bed and try to bite you, and you go, 'Nothing's changed!'

You opened and closed the production I saw with little children with masks on playing recorders. And of course, the big thing was the bags on the actors' heads. Why?

To me a play, or any art is just like the paintings on the cave walls that the first human beings did. Those poor fuckers were the first ones to experience being conscious. What a bizarre experience it is to know that we are alive. And wonder if there is a God, and will something save us? To be alive and to understand the existence of pain is pretty frightening. And all I'm doing is drawing myself, or just people, up on the wall of the cave, just to have a look and try to understand the mystery of being here on this big rock in the middle of a vast space we know nothing about. So whatever picture I make up there on the wall, or on the stage, is some aspect of how it feels to be alive. And just like those cavemen, I think the drive to do it is very primal.

I started writing that play before I got sick and I finished it afterwards. I had been in hospital in London for nine weeks. I had nearly died. Alcohol had almost destroyed my inner organs. I couldn't walk. I had basically tried to kill myself. Not consciously. But there was a drive deep inside me to finish my existence. It was uncontrollable and I was at its mercy. But something pulled me through. I survived and I made a full recovery. The bags on their heads represented my fear I suppose. And it was a pretty powerful image. Of course, the critics were all, 'I don't get it . . . ' Boo hoo. But people genuinely came up to me and spoke about the way that play hit them right in the gut. Sure, a lot of people were probably expecting something else. But that was how I was expressing myself at that time. And that's my job.

I was so lucky to have Jim Norton and Dearbhla Molloy. She was a revelation. I already knew Jim, and I knew he had the balls to do it. But she was so beautiful and had great poise and trusted me so much. A weird show. But a good one. It was done first as part of a triple bill in the theatre festival in Dublin, with one-act plays by Neil Jordan and Brian Friel. In itself, just being on the bill with those two was pretty incredible. Me and Neil were slightly like, 'What are we doing sharing a bill with Brian Friel?!' And Brian really delivered. His play, *The Yalta Game*, was a pure unadulterated pleasure from start to finish. Ciaran Hinds and Kelly Reilly, directed by Karel Reisz. Hard to beat. A cracker. I've been so lucky, the people I've been around.

You've been at it, let's say professionally, for about ten years now. I'm almost frightened to ask it, but what do you think you've learned in that time?

Carol, I'm as caught up in the middle of it as I ever was. I've learned probably very little. A few scraps or a few very basic things and that's it.

Like what?

When you put people in a room before a show there is already a huge amount of energy. If you are going to be mad enough to try to get everybody facing the same way and look at your work, you have to respect those people. And those people *want* to like what they are going to see. They don't want to hate it. And that energy humming in the room, before anything happens, is love. And you have to give your work to them with love and I hope I do. Once the show starts, you have to keep the love flowing.

I am compelled to do it. I'll probably never understand it, just like I know I will probably never understand myself, which is the hardest thing for anyone to understand. Like Aristotle says, 'Know thyself.' If you even get close to doing that, you are flying. I am nowhere near that place. Maybe I'll just give up at some point and try to enjoy my life without all the chest-beating and soul-searching – i.e. playwrighting! But for now I'm still just scratching those pictures up there on the wall, and people are still coming to sit and have a look. It's all I can do. And if they want to come, how can I not do it? You know? What else are we here for? Okay there are lots of people who probably think I'm rubbish or whatever. But what can I do? It's too late now. I've done it!